From Canberra to Harare
seven years in the life of the WCC

What has the World Council of Churches been doing since its seventh assembly in Canberra?

The brief articles in these pages try to answer that question. Together, they highlight the main issues on the WCC's agenda between 1991 and 1998 and describe some of the major activities undertaken to address them.

A survey of this type and length is a series of hints and pointers, a sketch rather than a detailed picture. Yet even these broad strokes give an indication of the breadth and diversity of the WCC's involvements.

Most of the work described here is carried out through the WCC's central offices in Geneva. These activities respond to mandates that come from the 330 member churches around the world who make up this fellowship.

The mandate of the WCC

The Council's core areas of concern are summarized in the list of functions in its Constitution. Proposals for how to address these take concrete shape in the WCC governing bodies. Chief among these is the assembly, every seven years, at which delegates from all member churches set the broad policies for the Council's programme until the next assembly.

The assembly elects 150 of its members to the Central Committee, which meets about once a year to review, assess and provide further guidance for the ongoing work of the staff. The Central Committee in turn appoints several commissions and other bodies which bring specific advice and expertise to particular areas of work. And the circle of people taking part in the Council's work is further widened through conferences, meetings and consultations, as well as encounters during WCC visits to churches, councils of churches and other organizations and groups.

The acid test for all the work of the WCC is its relevance to its member churches around the world. Is it meeting their needs? Does it match their expectations? Above all, does it enable, encourage and if necessary push them to take seriously the vocation they have acknowledged – to work together for the unity of Christ's church?

The background of any account of what the WCC as an organization is doing is thus formed by the everyday realities in which its member churches live, witness and pursue the sometimes difficult calling to make visible the unity of the church. Global political and economic developments, changes in the situations of its member churches and ecumenical initiatives in which the Council itself is not directly involved are thus essential elements of the story of the WCC during a given period of time.

Of course, any attempt to summarize this context briefly runs the risk of oversimplified generalizations, misplaced emphases and important omissions. With that caveat, however, it may be helpful to mention a few themes that were predominant in the context of the WCC's work between 1991 and 1998.

Many of these themes surfaced during the six meetings of the Central Committee between the Canberra and Harare assemblies. Sometimes they were reflected in public statements the Committee made, sometimes in reports it heard from its moderator and general secretary, sometimes in plenary presentations and discussions, sometimes in symbolic gestures.

Towards a common understanding and vision

Most of all, perhaps, an attempt to grasp the broader context for the life and work of the WCC animated the ongoing discussion "Towards a Common Understanding and Vision of the World Council of Churches" (CUV). Launched by the previous Central Committee in 1989, this process of study and consultation was on the agenda of every meeting of the Central Committee during this period.

The seriousness with which the Council's governing bodies, staff, member churches and ecumenical partners took this process reflected a consensus that the ecumenical movement – and with it the WCC – are passing through a time of transition. The context in which the WCC works today – the world situation, the situation in the churches and the situation in the ecumenical movement – differs radically from that of 1948, when the Council was founded. In the light of these changes, it is critically important to renew the

A joyful ecumenical worship in Soweto in 1991, during the first visit of a WCC delegation to South Africa for thirty years, a harbinger of the epochal changes in that country which led to the end of the apartheid system three years later.

Globalization has brought ever starker contrasts between wealth and poverty – as in these street scenes from Rio de Janeiro and Berlin.

churches' commitment to the movement and to the Council, based on a new articulation of their shared understanding of what the WCC is and vision of what it ought to be.

The scope of its subject matter meant that many of the earlier discussions of CUV were extremely diffuse. A clearer focus came once the Executive Committee decided in 1995 to concentrate the process on producing a major document to be used as a basis for the churches' recommitment to the WCC at the eighth assembly in 1998. In 1996 the Central Committee sent a first draft to member churches and ecumenical partners for reactions. Their responses, including more than 150 in written form, went into the preparation of a new draft, which the Central Committee adopted in 1997 as a policy statement, to be presented to the eighth assembly.

The CUV text reaffirms the Basis of the World Council of Churches. While it proposes a reformulation of the list of the WCC's constitutional functions and purposes, this new wording (to be submitted to the eighth assembly as a proposed constitutional amendment) clarifies the existing ones rather than radically changing them. The significant difference comes in a strong new emphasis on the original understanding of the WCC as a fellowship of churches and as a servant and instrument of the ecumenical movement. This implies that the Council should in future concentrate much more on relations with and among its churches, so that they come to understand the Council not as an external agency conducting programmes apart from them but as a body of which they are essential members. It also suggests a much greater and more coordinated sharing of tasks with ecumenical partners – a recognition not just that the WCC *cannot* do everything, but also that it need not and should not try to do everything.

After the cold war

A word increasingly heard in ecumenical discourse during the 1990s is "globalization": a vision of "one world" fostered by transnational and increasingly worldwide structures of economy, finance and communication. This is quite different from the vision of human unity advanced by the ecumenical movement, the CUV document says, and globalization thus poses a direct challenge to the churches:

> The cost... has been growing fragmentation of societies and exclusion for more and more of the human family. In their own international relationships the churches are under pressure to adapt themselves to this system and to accept its values, which tend to overlook if not deny the spiritual dimension of human life.

> The ecumenical movement has sought a distinctly different model of relationships, based on solidarity and sharing, mutual accountability and empowerment... All existing ecumenical structures must reassess themselves in the light of the challenge to manifest a form and quality of global community characterized by inclusiveness and reconciliation.

Some beneficiaries of globalization have spoken enthusiastically of a "new world order". This term already featured in the Canberra assembly statement on the Gulf War. Rejecting the version of a new post-cold war world order displayed in the decision to go to war in the Gulf, the assembly said it was rather time "to build a new world order of justice, the foundation stone of peace..., which ends the domination and exploitation of the poor by the rich".

The concerns raised by this assembly statement, especially over the weakening of the United Nations "as guarantor of a comprehensive international peace order", have remained on the Council's agenda. The 1995 Central Committee meeting included a substantial discussion of "global governance".

The aftermath of the Gulf War itself continued to preoccupy the WCC, particularly the sanctions imposed on Iraq and the repeated threats of US military intervention. The effect of the application of these sanctions on the Iraqi people was the occasion for the visit of an ecumenical team to Baghdad in January 1998.

The point of reference for this visit was the Central Committee's extensive 1995 memorandum on the use of sanctions. Prompting the WCC's concern at that time were not only the sanctions against Iraq, but also the international sanctions against Serbia and Montenegro and the US economic embargo of Cuba. The latter drew a special condemnation from the WCC in 1996 after the US Senate passed a measure to penalize other countries trading with Cuba.

The case of Serbia was more controversial for the WCC. The Central Committee's 1994 message to the churches in the former Yugoslavia referred to the suffering sanctions were causing Serbian civilians. The vigorous debate which that sentence aroused was one episode in a series of disagreements within the Council and its member churches over the protracted tragedy in those countries.

The conflict itself was made more bitter by the religious affiliations which were often used to inflame hatred between Serbs, Croats and Bosnian Muslims. Evidence of the depths – and profound historical roots – of these antagonisms were vivid at the Central Committee's very first meeting in 1991 during an open hearing addressed by a Serbian Orthodox bishop and a Croatian Catholic bishop. The WCC and Conference of European Churches (CEC) organized several high-profile meetings of religious leaders from the three sides, as well as channelling aid to victims of the war and helping to raise international awareness of the use of rape as a weapon in the war.

The organized abuse of women in this conflict shocked the world when reports of it (including one from a team sent by the WCC in the winter of 1992) were published. This left a terrible scar on the entire female population of the former Yugoslavia: pain, confusion and isolation for victims who survived, fear and horror for women in every community. To express ecumenical solidarity with women whose lives were plunged into such chaos and suffering, the WCC in 1993 launched the Ecumenical Women's Solidarity

Fund. Stressing woman-to-woman assistance, the Fund made it possible quickly to channel support to self-help projects set up at the grassroots level to rebuild the self-esteem, dignity and basic human rights of women throughout the former Yugoslavia. In five years, the Fund has supported over 100 such projects, benefiting some 55,000 women in Bosnia-Herzegovina, Croatia, Macedonia and Serbia.

The tragedy of Yugoslavia raised "fundamental ecumenical concerns", according to the Central Committee's 1995 message to the churches there: "What does mutual accountability require in such a situation? What balance is to be struck between the duty of churches to challenge one another with regard to what the gospel requires and our mutual responsibility for one another in the ecumenical fellowship? What is the role of confession, repentance and forgiveness in ecumenical relations? What is the proper relationship between church, state, nation and people…?"

Elsewhere in Eastern and Central Europe the aftermath of the end of Communist rule may not have been as violent as the breakup of Yugoslavia. But the resulting upheavals confronted the churches there and their ecumenical partners with considerable challenges. After fifty years of imposed atheism and international isolation, religious freedom was restored in Albania, and its reconstituted Orthodox church was welcomed into the WCC. In some countries, the process of coming to terms with the past and the future created sharp divisions within churches, sometimes calling into question their international ecumenical relations.

The tractor in which this man and his family fled from Bosnia-Herzegovina became their temporary home.

With CEC, the Council worked for reconciliation by bringing together religious leaders in the warring former Soviet republics of Armenia and Azerbaijan. And it joined with ecumenical partners, including the Russian Orthodox Church, to provide relief assistance in Chechnya.

Pointed questions were posed about the WCC's own involvement with these churches during their years under Communist rule, especially when intelligence agency files were made public which mentioned church leaders with international ecumenical connections. The most sensational allegations of Communist influence on the Council came in a widely distributed article in *Reader's Digest* in February 1993. Immediately after the appearance of the article, an extensive dossier of information regarding each of the charges was provided to member churches. The Council repeatedly explained its admittedly controversial pol-

The late Armenian Apostolic Church Catholicos Vasken I and Sheikh-ul-Islam Allahshukur Pasha-zadeh, chairman of the Board of Caucasian Muslims, sign a joint agreement on reconciliation in 1993. Seated left and right are Jean Fischer and Konrad Raiser, general secretaries of the Conference of European Churches and the WCC, which arranged this meeting in Montreux, Switzerland.

A Roma couple in Romania. The end of the cold war and moves towards European unity in the 1990s highlighted threats that the continent would divide along economic lines.

icy during those years of relating chiefly to official representatives of member churches in these countries, and noted that its own archives regarding those relationships were open to all qualified researchers.

Alongside the turmoil in Eastern and Central Europe came moves towards unity in Western Europe. The potential for a new division of the continent along economic rather than political lines was noted during the Central Committee's 1992 discussion of its resolution on the European Community (now the European Union). Acknowledging both the promise and challenge of what was happening, the resolution urged churches to speak boldly to European institutions about "poverty, economic inequities, refugees, migrants and asylum-seekers, racism, xenophobia and anti-Semitism, environmental issues and relationships with other European states and with the two-thirds world".

Conflicts and hopes

The year 1992, the 500th anniversary of the voyage of Christopher Columbus, evoked renewed reflection on the legacy of European colonialism and its consequences for the indigenous peoples of Latin America and the Africans whose ancestors were taken there as slaves. Churches and international ecumenical bodies were active in the difficult efforts to restore peace and rebuild shattered societies in Guatemala and El Salvador after years of devastating civil war.

Nowhere did civil war take so heavy a toll in human lives as Rwanda. For the ecumenical community, the shock and pain of the murderous conflict between Hutus and Tutsis which erupted in April 1994 was heightened by the realization that Rwanda was said to have the highest percentage of church members of any African country and by evidence of the complicity of some prominent church leaders in the massacres. The long and arduous task of relief, rehabilitation and reconstruction, in which the WCC has played an active role, is hampered by renewed outbreaks of violence and persistent signs that large-scale violence might be rekindled in neighbouring Burundi, perhaps engulfing the entire Great Lakes region of Africa.

Africa as a whole – and the role of its churches, with the support of the international ecumenical community – was a central concern of the WCC throughout this period *(see article, p. 28)*. The most dramatic change was obviously the end of the apartheid era in South Africa, celebrated by the historic meeting of the Central Committee in Johannesburg in January 1994.

Working with the All Africa Conference of Churches, the WCC continued its efforts to work for an end to years of civil war in Sudan. A Central Committee statement in 1997 called for the immediate restoration of democracy in Nigeria and drew special attention to the suffering of the Ogoni people from environmental destruction by international oil operations and brutal treatment by Nigerian security forces. The Ogoni situation had been the subject of a special report published by the WCC in November 1995.

In February 1998 the Executive Committee praised the work of Bishop Leslie Boseto of the Solomon Islands, one of the WCC's presidents, for a peaceful resolution of the long-running but little-known conflict on the island of Bougainville. In Asia, the conflict in East Timor was a continuing concern for the WCC, the Christian Conference of Asia and other ecumenical partners. The Council also maintained its support to Korean churches in their persistent efforts to reunify that divided country. However, in 1995 (the 50th anniversary of the partition), plans for a worship service in which North and South Korean Christians would be joined by international ecumenical representatives in the demilitarized zone had to be called off when the South Korean government withheld permission.

The ecumenical scene

Hopeful and disappointing developments marked the overall quest for the visible unity of the churches during the 1990s. While not directly involved in either negotiations for church union or the ongoing bilateral theological dialogues between official representatives of two churches, the Council monitors these ecumenical initiatives closely, periodically bringing together participants in them for a review and analysis of what is happening.

In South Africa, two of the racially divided churches of the Dutch Reformed family (black and mixed-race) united; but efforts to bring the white Dutch Reformed Church into this union have not yet born fruit. The "Together on the Way" process for uniting the two largest Reformed churches in the Netherlands and the country's small Lutheran church advanced, though the way was proving longer than some had hoped. Projects for achieving greater unity across denominational lines short of actual church union – especially at the level of local congregations – were discussed at a WCC-sponsored consultation of united and uniting churches in Jamaica in 1995. Protestant churches, especially in Europe and North America, took several steps towards closer fellowship. Pentecostal churches

Leaking oil in Ogoniland, Nigeria.

Looking out from the old slave docks during worship at the conference on world mission and evangelism, Salvador de Bahia, Brazil, 1996 (see p.20).

in the US moved to restore the unity between predominantly white and predominantly African American bodies which had characterized the movement when it began in the early years of the 20th century.

But the widely hailed results of two international theological dialogues involving the Roman Catholic Church suffered setbacks. The Vatican Congregation for the Doctrine of the Faith published a long-delayed assessment which called into question some of the agreements from the first series of international Anglican-Catholic dialogues; and resistance in several member churches obliged the Lutheran World Federation to postpone plans to celebrate a theological agreement with the Roman Catholic Church on justification at the LWF's ninth assembly in Hong Kong in 1997. LWF member churches were asked to give their responses to the joint declaration by May 1998; and on the basis of these responses it is hoped that a declaration can be signed by the LWF and the Vatican later in the year.

While the ecumenical partnership between the Roman Catholic Church and WCC member churches was strongly affirmed and exemplified by the Joint Working Group and evidenced in a cordial response to the CUV document from the Pontifical Council for Promoting Christian Unity, there were clear tensions between the Roman Catholic Church and WCC member churches during this period as well.

These were most prominent in the painful relations with Orthodox churches in the wake of the changes in Eastern and Central Europe and the Catholic understanding of the "new evangelization" needed in an undivided but secularized Europe. Conflicts over "uniate" or "Eastern Catholic" churches (which follow a basically Orthodox liturgy but are in communion with the pope) were not resolved despite an agreement by Orthodox and Roman Catholic theologians that uniatism is not an acceptable model of church unity. And Orthodox saw the restoration of Roman Catholic ecclesial structures in Russia, particularly the appointment of a bishop in Siberia, as failing to respect agreed canonical territories.

Four encyclical letters by Pope John Paul II drew extensive ecumenical commentary and response: *Centesimus annus*, which continued the tradition of Catholic social teaching begun 100 years earlier in *Rerum novarum; Evangelium vitae*, largely noted for its reaffirmation of the traditional Catholic stands on abortion and birth control; *Tertio millennio adveniente*, setting forth a jubilee celebration for the year 2000; and *Ut unum sint*, an encyclical on the ecumenical movement in which the pope proposed a dialogue on the central issue dividing the Roman Catholic Church from other Christian churches – the office of the papacy.

The role of the pope in the unity of the church was at the centre of the dismay expressed in many quarters over a 1992 letter from Cardinal Joseph Ratzinger to Catholic bishops. In it the president of the Congregation for the Doctrine of the Faith expounded "some aspects of the church understood as communion". Addressing the Central Committee in 1992, Emilio Castro, then WCC general secretary, described the letter as an ecumenical "cold shower", asserting that in its chapter on ecumenism this letter, though in itself an internal Catholic document, was in effect calling on other churches to return to the Roman Catholic Church – reverting to an old "model of unity" that seems to run counter to the Second Vatican Council.

The uniate churches' communion with the pope was not the only issue troubling the WCC's Orthodox member churches during this period. As noted earlier, the changes brought about by the new religious freedom for Orthodox churches in Eastern and Central Europe elicited increasingly vocal dissatisfaction with ecumenism in a number of them. Whether the most important factor here was in fact sharp differences over Christian teaching and practice, or misunderstandings and deliberate distortions of positions taken by ecumenical organizations, or fears of being over-

Unloading supplies for the influx of refugees from Rwanda at the Tanganyika Christian Refugee Service camp, Tanzania, 1994.

whelmed by outside (especially Western) influences, or internal struggles within the churches themselves, the situation challenged the WCC and other ecumenical bodies to engage in deeper and more patient dialogue with this family of churches. Nevertheless, the Georgian Orthodox Church announced in 1996 that it was withdrawing from the Council.

Orthodox unhappiness with ecumenism was not limited to the formerly socialist countries. During 1991 and 1992 most of the Orthodox churches in the US National Council of Churches suspended their membership, largely over their differences with some Protestant churches on issues of human sexuality.

Ecumenical Patriarch Bartholomeos, a member of the WCC Executive Committee until his election as patriarch, made several efforts to bring together the primates of the Eastern Orthodox churches and to heal divisions within a number of those churches. A dispute between the Ecumenical Patriarchate and the Moscow Patriarchate over parishes in Estonia temporarily overshadowed these efforts at intra-Orthodox unity. An initiative by the Standing Conference of Orthodox Bishops in America to move towards a single Orthodox church body in the US (where Orthodox membership is divided among an archdiocese of the Ecumenical Patriarchate, the Orthodox Church in America, whose independence is recognized by the Moscow Patriarchate but not the Ecumenical Patriarchate, and a number of smaller, ethnically rooted bodies) stalled.

Within the WCC, Orthodox representatives voiced persistent concerns over a number of issues: proselytism *(see article p. 19)*, the use of "inclusive language" to refer to God, the acceptance by some churches of homosexuality, and differences in eucharistic practice. The last of these was the subject of several long and painful debates in the Central Committee in connection with plans for worship at the

Harare assembly. In the end, it was agreed that an ecumenical eucharistic service would not be part of the assembly programme (as had been the case in previous assemblies), but that congregations of various traditions in Harare would be asked to invite delegates and others to share in their own eucharistic services on one of the Sundays during the assembly.

Behind all these concerns lay an increasing insistence by the Orthodox churches that the WCC's structures for participation and decision-making – indeed, its very "ethos" – are foreign to their tradition, with the result that the Council's agenda and activities are overwhelmingly determined by its Protestant member churches.

Though widely hailed, theological agreements promising to heal the 1500-year rift between the Eastern Orthodox churches and the Oriental Orthodox churches, which divided over questions of Christology following the Council of Chalcedon in 451, did not yet bear fruit in restored canonical fellowship. Several Oriental Orthodox churches chose new primates. After years of oppression under the Mengistu regime, the Ethiopian Orthodox Church was able to elect a new patriarch in 1992. WCC Central Committee moderator Aram Keshishian was elected catholicos of the Armenian Apostolic Church (Cilicia) after his predecessor, Karekin, became catholicos of the Armenian Apostolic Church (Etchmiadzin) on the death of Vasken I. Karekin had himself been vice-moderator of the Central Committee from 1975 to 1983.

Both in meetings with WCC officials and on other occasions over the past seven years, several Orthodox leaders have underscored that the tensions with the Council arising in their churches must be seen in the light of their commitment to and concern for the ecumenical movement. This was evident in the contributions made by several of these churches to the Common Understanding and Vision process. As the preface to the CUV policy document acknowledges, that text does not pretend to resolve all differences over key issues. No one doubts that a good deal of difficult discussion remains – including the effort to distinguish "theological", "cultural" and "procedural" issues, as a 1996 inter-Orthodox consultation observed.

By the time of the meeting of the Executive Committee in February 1998, there was evidence that such conversations had begun in earnest. During its four-day session, the Committee devoted substantial time to discussing the issue of Orthodox participation in the WCC. Among other things, its members heard the report of an official visit to the Russian Orthodox Church several weeks earlier by a six-member WCC team, headed by the general secretary, and urged that this process of dialogue continue, taking up in particular questions of the WCC's "structure, ethos, working styles and decision-making procedures".

Metropolitan Kirill of Smolensk told the Committee that what is needed is for the churches together "to embark on a journey to find a new vision – not just to respond to Orthodox concerns about the WCC but in order to be witnesses to the gospel in the 21st century, so that we may be one and the world may believe."

A baptism service at a newly built Russian Orthodox church in Novosibirsk, in Siberia.

Structuring the work of the WCC
the quest for integration

Between the Canberra and Harare assemblies the World Council of Churches went through two comprehensive processes of internal staff restructuring.

The first, adopted by the Central Committee in September 1991, divided the programmatic work of the WCC into four units: (I) *Unity and Renewal*; (II) *Churches in Mission: Health, Education and Witness*; (III) *Justice, Peace and Creation*; and (IV) *Sharing and Service*. In his task of ensuring "a pattern of collaboration and integrity" in the work of the Council as a whole, the general secretary was assisted by two deputy general secretaries (for programme coordination and for relations and communication), as well as four offices relating to the entire house: Management and Finance, Church and Ecumenical Relations, Inter-Religious Relations and Communication.

The programme units were mandated to work in a collaborative and integrated fashion. For both practical and historical reasons, the work of each unit divided into what were variously called teams, streams or desks. It is this structure which is largely reflected in the accounts of the WCC's work which follow.

The process of study and consultation "Towards a Common Understanding and Vision of the WCC" had been set in motion in 1989 partly in response to those who believed that a broader discussion of this type should precede any restructuring of the Council. While that conviction had not prevailed, the emphases which emerged as the CUV process evolved, combined with a significant drop in the Council's income, did lead to a second restructuring. In 1996 the Central Committee asked that "an overall alternative programme and management structure for the whole work of the Council" be developed "in the light of the CUV process". The following year it approved an initial outline for such a structure, to be put in place after the Harare assembly.

To promote the integration of work which had been sought but largely unachieved by the 1991 structure, the new plan treats the WCC staff as a single administrative whole with a unified budget, abolishing the unit structure and the distinction between "programme" and "support" functions. For practical reasons, the staff will be divided into four clusters, each made up of several teams, but the emphasis will be on integrated work – undertaken by members of several teams and clusters – on a realistic number of key priorities, which will be determined by the governing bodies, advised by a single Committee on Programmes.

The four clusters will be staffed by persons with experience in and particular responsibility for working on (1) the *issues and themes* with which the WCC is concerned, (2) the *relationships* it maintains, (3) *communication* and (4) *finance, services and administration*. The ongoing coordination of staff work will be the responsibility of a deputy general secretary and a staff leadership group, made up of the general secretary, his or her deputy and the directors of the four clusters.

As outlined by the Executive Committee in February 1998, the four clusters will be made up of the following teams:

Teams in the Cluster on *Issues and Themes*
Faith and Order
Mission and Evangelism
Justice, Peace and Creation
Education and Ecumenical Formation

Teams in the Cluster on *Relationships*
Ecumenical Relations
Regional Relations
Inter-Religious Relations and Dialogue
International Relations

Teams in the Cluster on *Communication*
Public Information
Publications and Documentation

Teams in the Cluster on *Finance, Services and Administration*
Finance
Income Monitoring and Development
Human Resources (Personnel)
House Services
Computer and Information Technology Services

NOTE: Several activities closely related to the WCC have governing structures which include partners outside the Council as well. Among these, the Ecumenical Institute in Bossey will be attached to the general secretariat. The Council will maintain its working relations with Action by Churches Together (ACT) and the Ecumenical Church Loan Fund (ECLOF) through the team on Regional Relations; and with *Ecumenical News International* (ENI) through the Communication cluster.

About the cover

Photo 1 (WCC/Chris Black): Street children at the conference on world mission and evangelism in Salvador de Bahia, Brazil, 1996. Photo 2: A worship service in the Baptist church of Yangon, Myanmar. Photo 3: Roque Santeiro, on the outskirts of Luanda, Angola, is said to be Africa's biggest outdoor market. Photo 4: Street vendors in Albania. Photo 5 (WCC/Jonas Ekströmer): A child soldier in Liberia. Photo 6: People living with AIDS near Chiang Mai, Thailand. Photo 7: The WCC Central Committee meeting in Johannesburg, 1994. Photo 8 (WCC/Catherine Alt): Indigenous people at the 15th session of the UN working group, 1997, march in celebration of the 20th anniversary of the first international NGO conference on indigenous peoples of the Americas.

Photos 2, 3, 4, 6 and 7 are by WCC staff photographer Peter Williams.

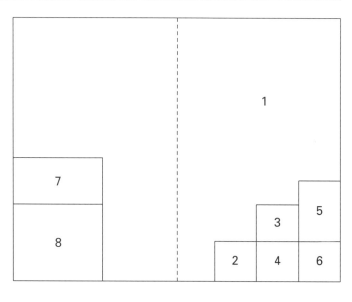

Members of the WCC Central Committee, 1991-1998

Presidents
Anna Marie Aagaard, *Evangelical Lutheran Church in Denmark*
Vinton R. Anderson, *African Methodist Episcopal Church* [USA]
Leslie Boseto, *United Church in the Solomon Islands*
Priyanka Mendis, *Church of Ceylon* [Sri Lanka]
Eunice Santana, *Christian Church (Disciples of Christ)* [USA]
Shenouda III, *Coptic Orthodox Church* [Egypt]
Aaron Tolen, *Presbyterian Church of Cameroon*

Officers
Aram I, *Armenian Apostolic Church (Cilicia)*, moderator
Soritua Nababan, *Batak Protestant Christian Church* [Indonesia], vice-moderator
Nélida Ritchie, *Evangelical Methodist Church of Argentina*, vice-moderator
Konrad Raiser, *Evangelical Church in Germany*, general secretary

Members (* indicates member of the Executive Committee)
Ruth Abraham, *Evangelical Church Mekane Yesus* [Ethiopia]
Charles G. Adams, *Progressive National Baptist Convention* [USA]
Ahn JuHye, *Korean Methodist Church*
Charles Ajalat, *Greek Orthodox Patriarchate of Antioch and All the East*
Levi Okang'a Akhura, *African Church of the Holy Spirit* [Kenya]
Ian E. Allsop, *Churches of Christ in Australia*
Mihaly Almasi, *Baptist Union of Hungary*
Ambrosius of Oulu, *Orthodox Church of Finland*
Andreas J. Anggui, *Toraja Church* [Indonesia]
Athanasios of Heliopolis and Theira, *Ecumenical Patriarchate of Constantinople*
Elias Audi, *Greek Orthodox Patriarchate of Antioch and All the East*
Paulo Ayres Mattos, *Methodist Church in Brazil*
Khushnud Mussarat Azariah, *Church of Pakistan*
Kathryn Bannister, *United Methodist Church* [USA]
Barbara Bazett, *Canadian Yearly Meeting of the Religious Society of Friends*
*Marion Best, *United Church of Canada*
André Birmelé, *Evangelical Church of the Augsburg Confession of Alsace and Lorraine* [France]
Karel Blei, *Netherlands Reformed Church*
Cristina G. Bösenberg, *Evangelical Church of the River Plate* [Argentina]
Nerses Hakob Bozabalyan, *Armenian Apostolic Church (Etchmiadzin)*
Violet S. Bredt, *United Church of Zambia*
*John H.Y. Briggs, *Baptist Union of Great Britain*
Edmond L. Browning, *Episcopal Church* [USA]
Ari Carvalho, *United Methodist Church* [USA]
Vsevolod Chaplin, *Russian Orthodox Church*
Gladys Chiwanga, *Church of the Province of Tanzania*
Chrysanthos of Limassol, *Church of Cyprus*
Chrysostomos of Peristerion, *Church of Greece*
Evanilza Loureiro Barros Correia, *Episcopal Anglican Church of Brazil*
Paul A. Crow, Jr, *Christian Church (Disciples of Christ)* [USA]
Kálmán Csiha, *Reformed Church of Romania*
*Daniel of Moldavia and Bukovina, *Romanian Orthodox Church*

Rosemary Davies, *Methodist Church* [UK]
Dometian of Vidin, *Bulgarian Orthodox Church*
Andrew Mbugo Elisa, *Episcopal Church of the Sudan*
Edeltraud Engel, *Evangelical Church in Germany*
Klaus Engelhardt, *Evangelical Church in Germany*
Erasmo Farfan Figueroa, *Pentecostal Mission Church* [Chile]
Walter Fejo, *Uniting Church in Australia*
Duleep R. Fernando, *Methodist Church* [Sri Lanka]
Julio Francisco, *Evangelical Congregational Church in Angola*
Olga Ganaba, *Russian Orthodox Church*
Maxine Garrett, *Moravian Church (Northern Province)* [USA]
*Virginia Gcabashe, *Methodist Church of Southern Africa* [South Africa]
Ato Wesen-Seged Gebreamlak, *Ethiopian Orthodox Tewahedo Church*
Milan Gerka, *Orthodox Church of Slovakia*
Hans Gerny, *Old Catholic Church of Switzerland*
Silva Ghazelyan, *Armenian Apostolic Church (Etchmiadzin)*
John Elliot Ghose, *Church of North India*
Wesley Granberg-Michaelson, *Reformed Church in America*
Makiko Hirata, *United Church of Christ in Japan*
Béalo Houmbouy, *Evangelical Church in New Caledonia*
Gregorios Y. Ibrahim, *Syrian Orthodox Patriarchate of Antioch and All the East*
Maryon P. Jägers, *Church of England*
Rosangela Jarjour, *National Evangelical Synod of Syria and Lebanon*
Jonas Jonson, *Church of Sweden*
*Margot Kässmann, *Evangelical Church in Germany*
Nangula Kathindi, *Church of the Province of Southern Africa* [Namibia]
Tusange Katonia, *Episcopal Baptist Community* [Zambia]
Ülle Keel, *Estonian Evangelical Lutheran Church*
Edea Kidu, *United Church in Papua New Guinea*
*Kirill of Smolensk, *Russian Orthodox Church*
Dimitre Kirov, *Bulgarian Orthodox Church*
*Leonid Kishkovsky, *Orthodox Church in America*
Wsiewolod Konach, *Autocephalic Orthodox Church in Poland*
George Koshy, *Church of South India*
Günter Krusche, *Evangelical Church in Germany*
Birgitta Larsson, *Church of Sweden*
Lavrentije of Sabac-Valjevo, *Serbian Orthodox Church*
Shirley Liddell, *Christian Methodist Episcopal Church* [USA]
Peter Lodberg, *Evangelical Lutheran Church of Denmark*
Janice Love, *United Methodist Church* [USA]
Kathy J. Magnus, *Evangelical Lutheran Church in America*
Jan Malpas, *Anglican Church of Australia*
David J. Mandeng ma Mbeleg, *Presbyterian Church of Cameroon*
Nadeje Mandysova, *Evangelical Church of Czech Brethren*
*Maryssa Mapanao-Camaddo, *United Church of Christ in the Philippines*
Hector Mendez Rodriguez, *Presbyterian Reformed Church in Cuba*
Donald E. Miller, *Church of the Brethren* [USA]
A. Matitsoane Moseme, *Lesotho Evangelical Church*
Irmela Müller-Stöver, *Evangelical Church in Germany*
John Mungania, *Methodist Church in Kenya*
Faith Mwondha, *Church of Uganda*
John R.W. Neill, *Church of Ireland*
Margarita Neliubova, *Russian Orthodox Church*

Nifon of Slobozia and Calarasi, *Romanian Orthodox Church*
Prakai Nontawasee, *Church of Christ in Thailand*
*Beatrice Odonkor, *Presbyterian Church of Ghana*
Christine Oettel, *Evangelical Church in Germany*
*J. Henry Okullu, *Church of the Province of Kenya*
Amos A. Omodunbi, *Methodist Church, Nigeria*
Joseph Omoyajowo, *Church of the Province of Nigeria*
Ruth Page, *Church of Scotland*
*Valamotu Palu, *Methodist Church in Tonga*
Park Jong-Wha, *Presbyterian Church in the Republic of Korea*
Tito E. Pasco, *Philippine Independent Church*
Constantin Patelos, *Greek Orthodox Patriarchate of Alexandria and All Africa*
Caroline Pattiasina, *Protestant Church in the Moluccas* [Indonesia]
Rachel Paulin, *Presbyterian Church of Aotearoa New Zealand*
Michael G. Peers, *Anglican Church of Canada*

Nenevi A. Seddoh, *Evangelical Presbyterian Church of Togo*
Serapion, *Coptic Orthodox Church* [USA]
Paul Sherry, *United Church of Christ* [USA]
Sri Winarti Soedjatmoko, *East Java Christian Church* [Indonesia]
Harrys T.M. Sumbayak, *Simalungun Protestant Christian Church* [Indonesia]
Bert A. Supit, *Christian Evangelical Church in Minahasa* [Indonesia]
Marianna Szabo-Matrai, *Lutheran Church in Hungary*
Jan Szarek, *Evangelical Church of the Augsburg Confession in Poland*
*Melvin G. Talbert, *United Methodist Church* [USA]
Kristine Thompson, *Presbyterian Church (USA)*
Timotheos, *Ethiopian Orthodox Tewahedo Church*
*Georges Tsetsis, *Ecumenical Patriarchate of Constantinople*
Eugene G. Turner, *Presbyterian Church (USA)*

Scenes from two of the six meetings of the Central Committee elected to govern the Council between the Canberra and Harare assemblies: in session at its historic gathering in Johannesburg in January 1994; and at the Place des Nations in Geneva in September 1995, demonstrating public opposition to the resumption of nuclear testing.

Victor Petliuchenko, *Russian Orthodox Church*
Elsie Philip, *Malankara Orthodox Syrian Church* [India]
Jean-Baptiste Rakotomaro, *Malagasy Lutheran Church*
Vidhya Rani, *United Evangelical Lutheran Churches in India*
*Birgitta Rantakari, *Evangelical-Lutheran Church of Finland*
Eberhardt Renz, *Evangelical Church in Germany*
Violet Rhaburn, *Methodist Church in the Caribbean and the Americas* [Panama]
Barry Rogerson, *Church of England*
John S. Romanides, *Church of Greece*
Heinz Rüegger, *Swiss Protestant Church Federation*
William G. Rusch, *Evangelical Lutheran Church in America*
José da Silveira Salvador, *Evangelical Presbyterian Church of Portugal*
Carlos I. Sanchez Campos, *Baptist Association of El Salvador*
Patricia Scoutas, *Ecumenical Patriarchate of Constantinople*

Anne L. Tveter, *Church of Norway*
Michel Twagirayesu, *Presbyterian Church of Rwanda*
Nove Vailaau, *Congregational Christian Church in Samoa*
Daniel Vanescote, *United Protestant Church of Belgium*
Angelique Walker-Smith, *National Baptist Convention, USA, Inc.*
Daniel E. Weiss, *American Baptist Churches in the USA*
Elizabeth Welch, *United Reformed Church in the UK*
Martin J Wessels, *Moravian Church in Southern Africa* [South Africa]
Aukje Westra, *Reformed Churches in the Netherlands*
Tungane Williams, *Cook Islands Christian Church*
*Zacharias Mar Theophilus, *Mar Thoma Syrian Church of Malabar* [India]
Maran Zau Yaw, *Myanmar Baptist Convention*
Nestor Zhiliaev, *Russian Orthodox Church*
Amosse Baltazar Zita, *Presbyterian Church of Mozambique*

The role of the church in the world
new questions and new approaches

A report presented by the Commission of the Churches on International Affairs to the Central Committee in 1996 observes that at no other time in its 50-year history has the WCC been obliged to struggle with such rapid, radical and fundamental change in international relations, or with such complex realities. As the churches and the Council move into a new century, the report suggests, profound changes are needed in the way they understand, reflect on and speak about the world around them. The limitations and distortions of "cold war thinking, based on the identification of an enemy and the confrontation of absolute good and evil" have become all too evident. Reality is seldom if ever so simple. "Good and evil, justice and injustice, righteousness and unrighteousness are omnipresent. What we are gradually discovering is that they are most often present together on different sides of disputes. We need a fresh approach."

Looking back on the years since the Canberra Assembly, the report poses a series of questions which outline the challenges to new thinking in international affairs. The following are some excerpts:

Violence and war
- What alternatives has the church to offer to violence as a response to conflict? What can the church do to lower or eradicate the incidence of violence in society?
- How can the churches and Christians strengthen their capacity to remain in dialogue on deeply divisive social and political issues?

Global governance
- In a time of widespread proliferation of complex, often competing and overlapping international institutions at world and regional levels, how can the church maintain sufficient distance to be able to reflect on what kind of institutions are needed today? How can we remain close enough to them to be able to influence their behaviour, promote constructive reforms and support conscientious and effective international civil servants who share our concerns?
- What could the churches do to ensure that the "voice of the peoples" is more effectively represented in the debates and the programmatic activities of the United Nations?
- What has the church to say about waning confidence in and the diminution of the power of the state?
- How can Christians and their churches exercise the responsibilities of citizenship vis-à-vis their own states and governments and at the same time retain the capacity to call them to accountability when they fail in their responsibilities?
- What roles do we see for "civil society" movements in the process of governance?
- How can civil society movements themselves be protected from the temptations of dogmatism and institutional rigidity?
- Will the churches, as they appeal for greater inclusiveness and democracy in the institutions of governance, apply the same critique to themselves and reform their own systems of government when they fail to meet the same standards?

Globalization
- How can the churches resist the forces of division and fragmentation today?
- As the forces of globalization put on the cloak of "internationalism" and even of "ecumenism", how can the church, the one body of Christ, make its understanding of universality heard? How can the ecumenical movement manifest in social and political terms the unity given in Christ and the sovereignty of God over all human powers?
- How is the moral voice of the church to be used in the face of such widespread economic, cultural and political immorality?"

Racism, ethnocentrism, nationalism
- What is the nature of the ecumenical fellowship and what does Christian unity require in a divided world?
- Does membership of the Council make churches accountable to and responsible for one another in such times?
- Can a church which fails to distance itself from and vigorously resist the use of violence by its own nation and people disqualify itself from WCC membership?

Confession, forgiveness, reconciliation
- What do we do when there is no "just" solution, when the "legitimate" claims for justice by the several parties to a conflict deny justice to the other?
- What moral criteria do we apply when judging the one and absolving the other is itself an act of injustice?
- How can the churches live out a model of caring and respectful dialogue which we can consistently apply and offer to others as an alternative?
- Can the churches learn a new way of looking at conflict which can enable us to see the humanity of people on all sides?
- What can the churches contribute to the shaping of new modes of thinking which take seriously the historical roots of conflict and approach it on its own terms, rather than on ours?
- Some of our absolutist statements of the past may have led us to miss opportunities to witness effectively in the present. How do we retain a prophetic voice and remain able to respond to crises which demand nuanced thinking and action?
- How can we oppose the granting of impunity for serious crimes against humanity in a way which can contribute to healing the wounds of history, and at the same time respond to the requirement of new democracies for stability in a time when the criminals of the past continue to wield power?
- How are truth-telling, impunity, forgiveness and reconciliation related?

* * *

The issues have become much more complex. Our tools of analysis need to be refined, and some corrected. How, in a time of deep moral crisis, can the church bring the moral voice of faith more consciously and effectively to bear in our actions and statements on public issues?

It is troubling that in precisely such a time many churches have become introspective, and tend to devote more of their attention and resources to their own institutional and confessional realities and pressing domestic concerns. The demands upon the church are great. How can the WCC encourage and enable the churches to maintain a sense of universal responsibility and exercise it more effectively?

Faith and Order

Unity and Renewal

The work of the programme unit on unity and renewal has brought together WCC activities addressing historic ecumenical concerns for theological study and dialogue, worship and spirituality, the laity and theological education.

The enthusiastic acclaim that greeted the appearance of the ecumenical text on Baptism, Eucharist and Ministry (BEM) in 1982 gave a new profile to the quest for church unity through intensive dialogue on specific issues of doctrine, church order and worship which have divided Christians.

Within the WCC, this work has been the major responsibility of the Faith and Order commission. Following the entry of the Roman Catholic Church into the ecumenical movement after the Second Vatican Council (1962-1965), it has also taken place through numerous bilateral theological dialogues between representatives of different church traditions.

In that sense, the BEM document did not come out of the blue. But its promising identification of wide-ranging "convergences" in these three areas of church life – familiar to every member and the source of so much division and conflict among Christians over the centuries – struck a responsive chord, challenging perceptions that the ecumenical movement and the WCC were mainly concerned with immediate and contemporary social and political issues.

During the 1980s churches around the world made their official responses to BEM – six volumes were eventually published by the WCC. The BEM document also had an important influence on ongoing bilateral dialogues, and a number of official agreements setting forth new relationships between specific churches drew extensively on it.

The responses to BEM, both official and unofficial, helped to clarify further some particular theological issues needing ecumenical study. The statement on "The Unity of the Church as Koinonia: Gift and Calling" by the WCC's Canberra assembly in 1991 and the deliberations of the Fifth World Conference on Faith and Order in 1993 (*see accompanying story*) offered further indications in this direction.

The centre of Faith and Order's work in the period since Canberra has thus been on four long-term studies. Each is a study in its own right, with its own processes of consultation, reporting and drafting, drawing on theologians and members of the Faith and Order commission. But they are understood to be interlinked. Exploring the interconnections among them and the implications of other earlier and ongoing studies for them has been the role of the Faith and Order staff.

The church as koinonia. The drafting group for this "ecclesiology study" has been working towards a convergence statement on the nature and purpose of the church, emphasizing the interrelatedness of faith, worship and witness.

Two other studies on specific topics are contributing to this effort. One has focused on recent developments in the understanding and practice of *episkopé* – the ministry of oversight as it has been understood within different Christian traditions. The other, undertaken in collaboration with the Institute for Ecumenical Studies in Strasbourg, has examined the relationship between baptism and the communion of the church.

Ecumenical hermeneutics. Behind the Faith and Order study on ecumenical hermeneutics, begun in 1994, lies the recognition that dialogues between churches are often complicated or even blocked by different ways of understanding and doing theology which are deeply rooted in their different cultural and confessional heritages.

An initial draft on this subject was sent to scholars in hermeneutics for comments; and two papers were commissioned to work out the hermeneutics that were implicitly at work in the BEM process. Further consultations have begun to develop a suggested set of guidelines for the drafting and interpretation of ecumenical texts in the light of the insights emerging.

Worship. The historic concern of Faith and Order with the relationship of worship to the unity of the church was the subject of two significant consultations during this period.

At a meeting in Ditchingham, England, in 1994 theologians and liturgical scholars investigated the variety that can flourish

Opening worship at the Fifth World Conference on Faith and Order, Santiago de Compostela, Spain, 1993, included the traditional censing of the altar in the Cathedral of St James by swinging the great "botafumeiro", suspended from the ceiling.

within a common pattern of worship. The title of the published report of this consultation – *So We Believe, So We Pray* – underscores the link between worship and church unity. Another facet of this relationship was explored at a 1997 consultation in Faverges, France, which focused on baptismal orders and the ethical implications of baptism.

Ecclesiology and ethics. Faith and Order undertook this study (*see accompanying story*), which involved three consultations between 1994 and 1996, in collaboration with the WCC's programme unit on Justice, Peace and Creation (Unit III). To follow it up, the Central Committee has called for further collaboration between these two parts of the WCC in two other projects: a new Faith and Order study on "Ethnic Identity, National Identity and the Unity of the Church" and the Unit III Programme to Overcome Violence (*see p. 25*).

The careful and necessarily slow process of these studies, which involve wide consultation and reflection, as well as the fact that some key terms ("ecclesiology", "hermeneutics", "koinonia", *episkopé*) tend not to be part of the everyday vocabulary of most church members, means that the work of Faith and Order does not attract immediate attention in many parts of the WCC constituency.

But one issue in which Faith and Order has been involved during this period did elicit some wider attention, even in the secular media. This grew out of a 1997 meeting in Aleppo, Syria, which produced a proposal for a possible solution to the centuries'-old anomaly that different ways of calculating the date of Easter mean that in most years this central festival of the church year is not celebrated on the same Sunday by all Christians.

Especially in the Middle East, but elsewhere as well, the phenomenon of two celebrations of Easter is especially embarrassing for minority Christian communities. The Aleppo proposal, to which a favourable Roman Catholic response has come from the Pontifical Council for Promoting Christian Unity, has rekindled hopes that agreement might be reached in this area.

SANTIAGO 1993

The Fifth World Conference on Faith and Order

Processions through the narrow, winding streets of Santiago de Compostela are not unusual. Pilgrims have long been drawn to this tourist centre in northwestern Spain whose cathedral is said to house the remains of the Apostle James.

Yet the procession leaving Santiago's Franciscan church on a warm Friday evening in mid-August 1993 was not an ordinary one. The several hundred people taking part were neither tourists nor conventional pilgrims seeking pardon or mercy. Rather, they had come from all over the world to take part in two weeks of intense theological discussion at the WCC's Fifth World Conference on Faith and Order.

The venue of the conference led many to speak of the ecumenical movement itself as a pilgrimage. For those seeking symbols of the distance covered since Faith and Order's previous world conference in Montreal 30 years earlier, holding the conference in so overwhelmingly Roman Catholic a setting was a striking one.

Only five Catholics had attended the Montreal conference, as

observers. In 1968, after the Second Vatican Council, the Roman Catholic Church became a full member of the Faith and Order plenary commission. Twelve of the commission's 120 members are now named by the Vatican; and the 32 Catholics registered in Santiago made up the fourth-largest confessional group (after Orthodox, Reformed and Lutherans).

In her opening address, Faith and Order commission moderator Mary Tanner of the Church of England noted how Faith and Order's work has been enriched not only by full Catholic participation, but also by a broader representation of Pentecostal and evangelical theologians, greater numbers of theologians from outside Europe and North America and a "more just" presence of women.

One task of the conference was to review what Faith and Order had done since 1963. The focus was on three major multi-year studies, each concentrating on one component of visible unity: common faith, common life, common witness.

– *Confessing the One Faith* is a contemporary ecumenical explication of the fourth-century Nicene Creed aimed at helping churches to recognize the one apostolic faith in their own lives and in the lives of others.

– The best-known of the three studies – *Baptism, Eucharist and Ministry* – is the search for what Tanner called "a sacramental life inseparable from the total life of discipleship in the ordinary stuff of everyday living".

– *Church and World* explores from the perspective of the kingdom of God the link between the nature of the church and its mission and service in the world.

In reports from the four sections in which the main work of the conference was done, delegates called for new or continued attention to several topics related to these studies. Among specific suggestions for further study:

– *apostolicity*: the question of how churches recognize "whether the risen Christ *we* know is present in the life of others";

WCC Faith and Order director Günther Gassmann with two speakers at Santiago 1993: Metropolitan John of Pergamon of the Ecumenical Patriarchate, and Anglican Archbishop Desmond Tutu of South Africa.

- *baptism*: can the churches' growing mutual recognition of each other's baptism have positive repercussions on other facets of the search for unity?
- *ordination of women to the ministry*: painful though it may be, ecumenical discussion of this must continue; meanwhile, "it would be helpful if churches would refrain from negative judgments on decisions either to ordain women or to continue a practice of not ordaining them";
- *the ministry of "oversight"*: while agreement is growing that the church needs such a ministry, differences persist on the issues of "personal bishops" and the "historic episcopacy";
- *primatial office*, especially the controversial issue of the papacy: one section suggested that Faith and Order begin a study of a "universal ministry of Christian unity" which would be "carried out in a pastoral way, speak for Christianity to the world at large and be bound to the community of all the churches and their leaders";
- *hermeneutics*: how churches can communicate with each other across barriers arising from their different theological methods, concepts and vocabulary – at a time when many people are utterly sceptical about the value of the whole enterprise.

The most all-encompassing study called for at Santiago was on "the nature of the church and the unity we seek" in the light of koinonia – the key term in the conference theme. As one section report acknowledged, the concept of koinonia, though often hailed as the most promising theme in ecumenical theology today, is not yet widely familiar beyond theological circles. Even translating it into contemporary languages is difficult (the English version of the conference message used "community, communion, sharing, fellowship, participation, solidarity").

Santiago described koinonia as "a gracious fellowship in Christ expressing the richness of the gift received by creation and humankind from God". This shared life of Christians is rooted in the Triune God – "the ultimate reality of relational life". Both unity and diversity must be safeguarded within the church: "difference is not a factor to exclude anyone from the koinonia of the church, especially when such differences are expressive of weakness or vulnerability."

Koinonia is inseparable from diakonia – Christian service to the whole world. The church is called "to share in the suffering of all, by advocacy and care for the poor, needy and marginalized, by joining in all efforts for justice and peace in human societies, by exercising and promoting responsible stewardship of creation and by keeping alive hope in the heart of humanity".

WCC general secretary Konrad Raiser told delegates that the world needs the churches' common witness, common action and visible unity more today than ever before. But "what we actually find is something quite different". Instead of living out the "impressive results" of theological convergence achieved ecumenically, the historic churches which formed the WCC seem to be retreating back into defining their own confessional identities according to their differences from others – even though these identities seem to elicit ever less loyalty from their members. And ecumenical dialogue itself has had little participation from the fastest-growing segments of Christianity – evangelical, Pentecostal and independent churches in the South.

Raiser called for constructive ecumenical dialogue aimed at better understanding of the integrity of the other, instead of trying "to dissolve the differences into consensus". Such a dialogue would see unity as a fellowship of those who continue to be different. "Rather than analyzing what still divides us, we should look instead at the already existing communion and try to deepen and expand it and make it manifest."

Ecclesiology and ethics

In the simplest terms, the WCC study on "Ecclesiology and Ethics", conducted by Faith and Order and the programme unit on Justice, Peace and Creation from 1992 to 1996, explored the link between what the church *is* and what the church *does*. Ecumenically speaking, this effort to hold together the issue of the nature and unity of the church with the common concern of the churches for ethical reflection and action aimed to heal the historic tensions between the "Faith and Order" tradition of seeking unity by working through doctrinal and theological differences and the "Life and Work" tradition of achieving unity by joining together to address social issues.

The heart of the study process was three consultations – at Rønde, Denmark, in 1993, Tantur, near Jerusalem, in 1994, and Johannesburg, South Africa, in 1996. These in turn produced three reports: *Costly Unity, Costly Commitment* and *Costly Obedience*.

Asylum-seekers, like these in a church in Germany, raise questions about what the church is and what it does.

The sequence of these three titles points to the progress made in both ecclesiological and ethical reflection during the four years: from a realization that "the unity we seek" will turn out to be *costly*, through a recognition that such unity will require *commitment* to one another, to an acknowledgment that all this has less to do with programmes and institutions than with *obedience* to the calling to be one and to serve all humanity and creation.

Two overarching convictions guided the study as a whole. The first is that ecumenical ethical reflection and action are inherent in the very nature and life of the church – and are thus inseparable from ecclesiology. The second is that ecclesiology and ethics must remain in dialogue, learning from each other despite their differences in vocabulary and in ways of looking at issues.

The Rønde consultation began by trying to relate two prominent concepts in recent WCC discussion: "koinonia", the key term of the Faith and Order statement on unity adopted by the Canberra assembly, and "justice, peace and the integrity of creation" (JPIC), the focus of the ecumenical social reflection which carried on the Life and Work tradition through the 1980s. The affirmation in the Rønde document that "the church not only *has*, but *is*, a social ethic, a koinonia ethic" laid the groundwork for the study as a whole, by insisting that ethical reflection must be done within the theological and ecclesiological circle. Thus Rønde sought to reflect ecclesiologically on "covenant" and "conciliarity", two key terms which the JPIC process had approached mainly through ethical categories. It reopened the question of the "ecclesial" significance of groups and movements working for justice, peace and environmental concerns; and it introduced into the ecumenical ecclesiological discussion the idea of the church as a "moral community".

The ecclesiological significance of ethical reflection and action was the focus of the Tantur consultation. Tantur insisted that it is not simply ethical reflection and action, but *ecumenical* ethical reflection and action, which are intrinsic to the church. It related the theme of "covenant" to both eucharist and ecumenical engagement. Picking up again the controversial question of how issue-oriented groups and movements are related to the church, Tantur suggested that while the term "koinonia" is best limited to those who understand themselves to be linked with the memory and message of Jesus Christ, an "important sense of community" may be generated and prophetic signs of the reign of God may also appear within groups whose motivation is not Christian. This in turn "may have implications for the way we understand the church". Finally, Tantur explored one particular expression of the church's identity as a "moral community", namely "moral formation" – the training in Christian discernment and ethical decision-making which happens not only through formal instruction but also through the whole life and worship of the church.

Moral formation within the wider context of the ecumenical movement was then the focal issue at the Johannesburg meeting. Its report warns of *mal*formation: the way in which the systems and structures of the world ceaselessly "instruct" us in its values and impose its priorities on us. The recovery and strengthening of Christian identity is thus a central task of Christian moral formation today, though the church as human institution is itself not immune from malformation. Johannesburg also developed the earlier emphasis on worship by focusing on baptism and the eucharist as contexts of formation.

While the study on Ecclesiology and Ethics has ended (the three reports and some interpretative essays were published in a single volume by WCC Publications in 1997), the real significance of the process will become clearer as Christians and churches consider its results and test them through their own experience.

Lay participation towards inclusive community

When the WCC was restructured after the Canberra assembly, one of the areas of work in the programme unit on Unity and Renewal was given the title "Lay Participation Towards Inclusive Community". That reflected the re-emergence of an old ecumenical concern on the WCC agenda.

Much of the stimulus and energy for the 20th-century movement for church unity came from dedicated Christians who have sought to live out their faith in areas of life other than the ordained ministry. The WCC staff thus included a Department of the Laity for many years; and the questions Christians were raising as a result of their engagement in various "secular" professions provided a dynamic element in the programming of the WCC's Ecumenical Institute in Bossey.

Meanwhile, most notably in Germany but also elsewhere, lay academies and lay centres of various types were being formed. Some have specialized in education and study, others are concerned with spiritual growth, still others are engaged in action in society. Even during the years when no desk in the WCC was explicitly identified with the laity, the Council actively helped to coordinate regional and global networks of these centres and to organize regular Courses for Lay Leadership Training around the world.

The most recent such course was held during February 1998. Following brief visits to lay centres in South Africa, Zambia and Zimbabwe, participants gathered in Harare for an intensive three-week period during which they identified three focal areas in which lay centres can confront what

A leadership training course in Johannesburg.

they called the "chains of hopelessness" in today's world – awareness-building (the role of the laity in education), service in society and community-building.

A world convention of Christian lay centres, held in Montreat, North Carolina, USA, in September 1993, underscored the renewal of attention to the laity issue within the WCC; indeed, the keynote address by WCC general secretary Konrad Raiser spoke of moving "towards a new definition of the profile of the laity in the ecumenical movement". To prepare themselves, most of the 300 participants spent the week before the conference as guests of one of the lay centres across the USA and Canada. The convention itself offered further opportunities to hear first-hand reports of how lay centres in every part of the world are – in the words of the theme – "weaving communities of hope".

Translating the new enthusiasm for the ministry of the laity which was evident in the Montreat convention into specific WCC programmes presented several challenges.

The dimension of inclusive community has been central. Thus the accent is not so much on what came to the fore in the early days of the WCC – equipping individual Christians for their "professional" activity "in the world" – but rather on the participation of everyone in the community as a whole. Within the Council itself, then, the laity concern can be seen more as a way of carrying out all programmes than as a programme in itself.

Emphasis has thus been given to the ecclesiological dimensions of the laity issue. There are evident ambiguities of language and differences of theological understanding to be clarified if churches are to understand each other when they speak of "the people of God as inclusive community".

An obvious point of continuing discussion is the distinction within the church between those who are ordained or set aside for a specific ministry of word and sacrament and those who are not. In its section on ministry, for example, the WCC's well-known 1982 document on *Baptism, Eucharist and Ministry* devotes almost all of its attention to the ordained ministry. But how can the distinction between "laity" and "clergy" be seen as complementary rather than exclusive?

Another important issue arising in recent discussion has come from the recognition that the notion of being the people of God is an important element of the identity of Jews and Muslims. What are the implications of this interfaith dimension of what has become a key term in Christian identity as well?

These issues were addressed in a process of study and consultation over several years in response to a mandate from the Central Committee in 1994. Theological reflections were solicited from persons both within and outside of WCC circles, including a member of the Pontifical Commission on the Laity. A survey was undertaken among WCC staff; two research papers were prepared; and several small meetings offered an opportunity for focused discussion of specific points of concern.

Out of all this emerged the agenda for a major consultation "Towards a Common Understanding of the Theological Concepts Laity/Laos: The People of God", held in Geneva in May 1997. The 27 participants addressed two major issues: the relationship between the church and the world and the relationship between the clergy and the laity.

The concluding statement of the consultation notes that "the 'laity' constitutes 98 percent of the church in its life of worship and service. The laity are the agents of Christ in the world, daily missionaries. The *laos* is the common element between the life of the congregation and the life of the world. The laity are the church in the world."

The emphasis on *inclusive* community in the WCC's renewed attention to the laity acknowledges that the differences, distinctions and divisions present in the church – no less than in society as a whole – may lead to the exclusion of certain persons and indeed entire categories of people from meaningful participation and fellowship.

Among those often excluded from full participation in the life and work of the church are persons with disabilities. For two years a consultant worked with the Geneva staff to establish relations with those addressing this issue in churches, councils of churches and agencies around the world. Four groups of priorities were established:

theology, peace and justice, awareness-building, and research and evaluation.

Consultations were held in Beirut in 1995 ("From Institutionalization to Independent Living", organized with the Middle East Council of Churches), Seoul in 1996 ("Theological and Sociological Approach to the Differently Abled", organized with the National Council of Churches in Korea and the Christian Conference of Asia), and Sibiu, Romania, in 1996 ("The Church as Inclusive Community: The Place and Role of Differently Abled Persons in its Life, Education and Mission", organized with the WCC desks on education and on Orthodox studies in mission).

A policy document on the theological and sociological understanding of the issue of disabilities was received by the Central Committee in 1997. But it has not proved possible to find funds to convert the consultancy into a permanent programme for the WCC.

Worship and spirituality

Having heard much about WCC concerns and actions in the area of the churches' engagement in social issues, many people attending their first WCC conference or assembly are surprised by the extensive time and attention given to worship. Often participants say later that the worship ranked among the high points of the meet-

ing for them. Prayer and spirituality have in fact always been an essential dynamic of the ecumenical movement; indeed, one of the earliest organized expressions of the ecumenical vision was the Week of Prayer for Christian Unity.

A WCC consultation on "Christian Spirituality for Our Times", held in Iasi, Roma-

A morning worship at the WCC's seventh assembly in Canberra in 1991.

A guitar accompanies the choir in this Episcopal Church in a small town of Western Equatoria, Sudan.

nia, in 1994, emphasized the importance of holding together the "inward and outward journeys of faith":

> In the midst of ethnic hatred and demonic violence, we dare to hope in a radical love that accepts and even prays for one's enemies, and reaches out to all those defined as "the other". Faced with a lethal assault on the earth's capacity to sustain life, we proclaim a reconciliation which unites us with the goodness of God's creation and restrains self-destructive greed. Encountering millions whose very lives are placed on the margin of life, we are rooted in a love that is fiercely intolerant of global inequity, and we seek nourishment from bread which can be shared by all.

That dimension of "spiritual ecumenism", underscored in the Second Vatican Council Decree on Ecumenism, is evident in many of the portraits of "ecumenical pilgrims" collected in a book under that title published with the collaboration of the Worship and Spirituality stream in 1995.

It is no easy task to bring the unifying element of prayer to life in the setting of ecumenical worship. Understandings of how to pray vary from tradition to tradition – some using prayers from a book, some using free prayers, some praying in tongues, some valuing silence.

While many people are eager to refresh their own worship with new words, music, symbols and gestures coming from a wide range of traditions, many others are uneasy with forms and styles of worship different from those with which they have grown up.

Considerations such as these have been prominent on the agenda of regional worship workshops which the Worship and Spirituality stream has organized over the last seven years. They arise not so much in theoretical discussions as in immediate practical ways.

For example, participants in an African

For many persons who attend a WCC meeting, worship services often provide the most memorable moments.

---

workshop in Malawi in 1992 shared lively and spirited African rhythms and songs – which then had to be fit into worship structures identical to those of North America or Europe. To find a picture of Jesus as an African in African dress, they had to journey many kilometres to a Roman Catholic Church. One local participant said that Muslims coming to Malawi were claiming that Christianity is a white religion and that one need only look at the pictures of Jesus in the churches to see that this is the case.

On the other hand, a Latin American worship workshop in Rio de Janeiro several months later had a quite different experi-

ence. Participants attended a Catholic worship service in a *favela* where the congregation claimed their freedom by dancing to Afro-Brazilian rhythms and celebrating the life of slave woman who had refused to submit to the advances of her Portuguese master.

Ideas from these worship workshops are one of the sources for a growing collection of materials in the WCC's Worship Resource Centre. The old and new materials assembled here constitute a rich treasury not only for worship services at WCC gatherings but also for member churches.

The WCC's worship services are in fact a way of sharing liturgical materials across cultures and traditions. Participants take the worship services home and adapt them in their own congregations or denominational meetings. Songs and prayers learned at ecumenical gatherings later find their way into new hymnals, worship books and prayer calendars.

Other partners are carrying this forward in various places around the world, and are beginning to form a network which keeps the Worship and Spirituality stream in touch with its sources.

Some of the work done by the stream was gathered together in the 1996 publication *Worshipping Ecumenically*, a resource book designed to help planners of local ecumenical gatherings to adapt ecumenical worship services to their own particular context. The book also offers practical guidelines for making ecumenical worship effective and explains some of the obstacles and pitfalls that must be taken into account.

Ecumenical theological education

Under the successive names "Theological Education Fund", "Programme on Theological Education" and "Ecumenical Theological Education", the concern with how the churches are training their ministers has been on the WCC's agenda for nearly 40 years.

The roots of this lie in the churches' missionary outreach. The Theological Education Fund was established in 1958 by the International Missionary Council, prior to its 1961 merger with the WCC; and the major concern in the early years was providing human and material resources to enable newly independent churches, many of them in newly independent countries, to train their own ministers.

From the outset, its two focal points were stimulating churches to develop their theology, mission and education in ways appropriate to their own immediate situations (contextualization) and helping churches to achieve financial stability for their theological institutions and ministerial training programmes.

Inevitably, the accent came to fall on churches and theological institutions in the South. Partners from Europe and North America were seen as contributors, providing financial support as well as human resources, especially in the form of short-term guest professors. Over the years, however, there has been a growing effort to make northern churches and theological institutions genuine partners in ecumenical dialogue rather than mere donors.

Adopting the name Programme on Theological Education in 1978 was a way of indicating that although the element of funding cannot be ignored, it is secondary to generating in theological institutions visions that will foster the unity and mission of the church.

Through the 1980s two themes were important for the WCC's work in this area: theology *by the people*, recognizing that ministry is not the task of only one professionally trained group within the church, and *spirituality*, seeking to release theology and ministry from captivity to the academy and to make theologians and ministers more conscious of the obligation of obedience to the will of God.

All these facets have continued to be part of the work of what is now called Ecumenical Theological Education (ETE). But during the period since the Canberra assembly a widespread sense that we are at a critical juncture in the history of the churches, the ecumenical movement and the WCC led to a specific focus on the *viability* of theological education and ministerial formation.

The central question is: can the churches' programmes and processes for theological education and ministerial formation serve to renew and transform the lives of their students, their congregations and their societies? In other words, can these activities enable the people of God to be the people of God in their particular place and time? And if so, how?

Behind this lay two perceptions: a widely negative image of theology, which few people, even faithful church members, look upon as a lively and dynamic instrument for renewal; and the limited success of efforts so far to encourage theological education that is genuinely ecumenical.

For two-and-a-half years, ETE solicited reflections on these issues from church representatives, educators and theologians around the world. At the same time it organized eight regional consultations on viability, culminating in a global consultation held in Oslo in August 1996.

The 130 participants at the Oslo meeting identified several achievements of the WCC's work in theological education over the years: the encouragement of reform of ministerial formation, the support for faculty development and self-reliance of theological institutions in the South, the promotion of an ecumenical curriculum for theological education, the networking among regional associations of theological schools and the challenges posed and stimulus given to traditional theological faculties in the North.

They noted that a new dimension has emerged in ecumenical theological education as a result of the growing visibility of women in theology and ministry, taking shape around the world in new groups and networks of women theologians. They reflected on the need to revitalize Theological Education by Extension and similar decentralized programmes as an essential component of realizing the vision of "theology by the people". And they discussed what role ecumenical theological education might have among Pentecostal, charismatic and indigenous Christian movements arising in Africa and elsewhere.

Thus while much progress has been made, the Oslo meeting said, ecumenical theological education remains an urgent and highly relevant concern. These tasks must continue to be addressed through the WCC, so that the global network of institutions for theological education is kept in touch with the ecumenical vision of the church and its mandates for unity, mission and justice.

Viable theological education is an essential concern of churches everywhere – in Russia, where a staff member uses a computer to prepare a course in an Orthodox institute; in the study room at the Church of Melanesia Training Centre in the Solomon Islands; in a classroom setting at Nungalinya, a theological college for Aboriginal people in Darwin, Australia.

Mission and evangelism in unity

Churches in Mission: Health, Education, Witness

The work of the programme unit on churches in mission has covered three traditional concerns growing out of the missionary endeavours of the church: evangelism, Christian education and health and healing.

The description of the world missionary conference in Edinburgh in 1910 as the birthplace of the ecumenical movement reflects the central role which those involved in the mission of the church played in stimulating the search for visible Christian unity. In 1961, the International Missionary Council, which grew out of the Edinburgh conference, merged with the World Council of Churches; and mission and evangelism has been a key item on the agenda of the WCC since then.

But the WCC – which is a fellowship of churches and not a church – does not itself send out missionaries or engage in mission. Its task is rather to help churches to fulfill their own missionary calling, to reflect with them on the problems and questions that arise in doing so and, above all, to encourage them to maintain the link between the mission and the unity of the church.

A major obstacle to strengthening the connection between mission and unity is the fact that, as WCC Evangelism Secretary Samuel Ada puts it, "the churches were built and have grown for years in the spirit of competition. It is natural that evangelism, the principal instrument of this building and growing, is jealously kept as an internal and private resource by every community."

So long as a church sees its missionary engagement, in particular evangelism, only in terms of increasing its own membership rolls, it will have little inclination to consider witnessing together with other churches.

During the 1990s that unhappy reality has been all too evident in many of the formerly socialist countries of Eastern and Central Europe, where newly recovered religious freedom has opened the way to a stream of evangelizing groups from outside. These activities often ignore or deliberately by-pass existing local churches, who see them as an effort to steal their members. In response, the WCC has devoted extensive attention during this period to the question of common witness and proselytism; and two major texts have appeared: a study document from the Joint Working Group between the WCC and the Roman Catholic Church, and a statement commended to WCC member churches by its Central Committee in September 1997 (*see accompanying story*).

This competitive face of evangelism is not only a matter of incoming missionaries. In Africa, Christianity is growing most rapidly, Ada notes, "in the communities that affirm strongly that God solves instantly the problems of the faithful. In the historic churches that teach other forms of the presence of God, the number of members either remains constant or is improving slightly."

That challenges the historic churches to review their theology and practice of evangelism.

Given these temptations to engage in mission that works against unity, how can the WCC help the churches to hold the two together? Clearly the time is long past when the answer to that question took the form of agreements among churches to divide up responsibilities for unevangelized territories in order to spread their resources and stay out of each other's way.

The heart of the work of the Evangelism Desk involves building and strengthening a network of persons responsible for evangelism in their own churches and mission organizations.

This Evangelism and Witness Network now consists of some 250 people around the world. The information they provide the WCC about what the churches are doing in evangelism is in turn disseminated more widely through the *Ecumenical Letter on Evangelism*, which is published four to six times a year and serves as a forum for reflection on key contemporary mission issues.

A main method of work for the Evangelism Desk has been holding small consultations which bring together persons responsible for mission and evangelism in a region or country, in cooperation with regional or national ecumenical bodies. Consultations have been organized on "The Fire on the

Religious literature being sold outside the Baptist church in Yangon, Myanmar.

Horizon – A Call to Evangelism" (Africa), "Called to Common Witness" (Asia), "Evangelism in Cuba Today" and "Voicing the Gospel in the Pacific".

Building and strengthening networks with specialized mission constituencies has also been a focal point of the work of the other desks in the team on mission and evangelism in unity.

A desk on Orthodox Studies and Relations in Mission has enabled the WCC both to take account of the particular mission insights of the Orthodox churches and to confront the special challenges these churches face in their mission. Similarly, the presence of a consultant representing the Roman Catholic missionary orders, seconded by the Pontifical Council for Promoting Christian Unity, has helped to enrich ecumenical mission reflection with information and insights from the mission activities of the world's largest church, which is not a member of the WCC.

In addition, a programme on studies and education in mission has made possible

Outdoor evangelism on a street in Lagos, Nigeria.

encounter and exchange among churches in the area of educational methodology. Typifying this approach were two encounters in 1996 involving the Association of Christian Lay Centres in Africa, the Rural Libraries and Resources Development Programme in Zimbabwe and the Finnish Ecumenical Learning Association.

The theme of these two learning events was "Called to Be Caretakers of the Earth"

– one of the four areas of reflection at the WCC's 1989 world mission conference in San Antonio. The first took place in Limuru, Kenya, and concentrated on experiential learning in the area of the environment; the second was held in Hauho, Finland, and enabled the participants to examine the same topic in a different cultural context, with a view to helping them to become teachers in their own context.

Common witness and proselytism
the search for responsible relationships in mission

"Conversion" is a theme which has attracted considerable attention in ecumenical circles since the WCC's seventh assembly; and the image of turning implied in the biblical idea of conversion is explicit in the theme chosen for the eighth assembly: "Turn to God – Rejoice in Hope".

The Groupe des Dombes, the French ecumenical study group noted for its pioneering work in Protestant-Catholic dialogue, released a widely-hailed theological study which phrased the ecumenical imperative in terms of the *conversion* of the churches (an English translation was published by the WCC in 1993). The WCC's journal *The Ecumenical Review* devoted an issue to the subject of conversion. At the 1992 Central Committee meeting, retiring general secretary Emilio Castro focused his final report on the topic, and his newly elected successor Konrad Raiser described his own ecumenical engagement as a kind of "second conversion".

But the call to conversion is by no means ecumenically uncontroversial. The late Greek Orthodox patriarch Parthenios of Alexandria and All Africa, a WCC president, put his finger on the point of tension in responding to Castro's address. While praising Castro for offering a "guide to the real problems of our struggle for the unity of the churches", Parthenios raised an old issue that makes conversion "a difficult and dangerous word" – namely, proselytism.

Fear and anger about foreign missionaries who use various forms of coercion to "convert" people from one Christian church to another is a special, though not unique, concern in countries where Orthodoxy is the predominant Christian tradition. A passionate discussion during a presentation of WCC diaconal

work at the same Central Committee meeting made that clear.

Margarita Neliubova of the Russian Orthodox Church told the Committee that while the churches in her country were very grateful for "the support of their brothers and sisters from other churches in the present difficult situation, there are forms of help and aid that are not acceptable for our churches, where the sharing turns into dividing."

The intentions of missionary groups coming to Russia from outside may be good, she acknowledged, "but often they do not see that our country is not the spiritual desert they expect. There are large and strong Christian churches which have survived oppression and persecution, churches deeply rooted in the history and culture of the people. These churches are experiencing a difficult financial situation, as the whole country is, but they are strong enough to fulfill their vocation and respond to the new challenges they are facing."

One foreign mission group in Russia hired a 60,000-seat stadium and advertised a rally at which food parcels and Bibles would be given away and people baptized. "I know it is expensive to hire a sports stadium," Neliubova said. "We don't need an *expensive* mission but a *costly* one, which unites and does not divide."

Olga Ganaba added that because of the widespread poverty in Russia, "everything coming to the people means something. They don't think about what is good about our country. They conclude that people live better in the West, so the church must be better there too."

Dimitre Kirov from the Bulgarian Orthodox Church spoke of a "mass invasion" of his country by groups "who have no the-

Mormons from the USA are sent abroad on two-year missionary service; these two young men are calling at a home in Georgetown, Guyana.

ology and promise miracles" and take advantage of the fact that "in the past forty years our population has not been religiously educated".

From outside Eastern Europe, Coptic Orthodox Bishop Serapion said his own church had faced similar situations with foreign missionaries in Egypt. "We may complain about their coming," he said, "but we cannot prevent them. The only way we could stand was to revive our own churches." Khawlhring Lungmuana spoke of new church divisions arising in India as "evangelical" congregations leave "mainline" churches, then send out their own missionaries with financial support from abroad.

The WCC's firm opposition to proselytism has been expressed in a number of official statements over the years. But the issue was placed back on the Council's agenda both because of the intensity of feeling aroused by the new situation in the formerly socialist countries and explicit concerns that some of the offending mission activity there was coming not from independent fundamentalist groups but from WCC member churches.

A series of consultations in various forums was undertaken, with a special effort to involve representatives of both those who consider themselves targets of proselytism and those accused of proselytizing activities, including some groups not affiliated with the WCC. The Joint Working Group between the WCC and the Roman Catholic Church issued a new report on common witness and proselytism; and the issue was also taken up at the 1993 world conference on Faith and Order and in the preparations for the 1996 world conference on mission and evangelism. It featured prominently in WCC discussions with Orthodox church leaders.

In 1997 the WCC Central Committee commended a new statement on the subject to the churches. Although it condemns proselytism in no uncertain terms as "a perversion of authentic Christian witness and thus a counter-witness", the title of the statement "Towards Common Witness", reflects its intention to move beyond denunciations to a challenge to responsible mission relations that promote authentic common witness in which the gospel is seen as relevant in the world today.

The statement acknowledges that "some people may move from one church to another out of true and genuine conviction… as a free decision in response to their experience of the life and witness of another church". But it warns sharply against encouraging such moves through tactics like unfairly criticizing the beliefs and practices of another church, presenting one's own church as "the *true* church", taking advantage of problems in another church to attract members to one's own, offering humanitarian aid to induce people to join another church, or taking advantage of people's lack of education, loneliness or illness to "convert" them.

The statement includes a set of guidelines for "responsible mission" and suggests some practical ways of carrying these out.

The world conference on mission and evangelism

"Called to One Hope – The Gospel in Diverse Cultures" was the theme of the WCC's conference on world mission and evangelism, which brought some 600 people from almost 100 nations to Salvador de Bahia, Brazil, in late November 1996.

The ten-day conference, whose participants came from about 160 of the WCC's member churches, was the eleventh in a series which began in Edinburgh in 1910. These have been organized by the WCC since its 1961 merger with the International Missionary Council (the previous conference was held in San Antonio, Texas, in 1989).

The Salvador gathering was the culminating point in an intensive four-year study process among WCC member churches, related councils, mission agencies and academic and study centres in about 60 countries. The underlying theme for reflection was "Gospel and Cultures" – the challenges posed by the different ways in which the gospel takes root in and is illuminated by different human cultures, as well as the critique that the gospel brings to every human culture.

The concluding message from conference participants affirmed the need for Christian mission and expressed a prayer "that many will share with us in being called to one hope". But it also acknowledged that the history of Christian mission has too often demonstrated total insensitivity towards the cultures to which missionaries have been sent, bringing harm and pain to their peoples.

On the way to Salvador, the study process itself had involved numerous smaller consultations and generated a considerable number of publications, including a series of 18 pamphlets published by the WCC and examining how the gospel has taken root in many specific cultural settings around the world. One of the preparatory consultations, which brought together indigenous people from around the world, took place in Salvador itself just before the main conference.

The conference was structured in four parts, intended to provide "exposure, encounter, exploration and engagement".

Exposure came through the "Rainbow Festival of Gospel in Cultures", a large exhibition area where booths and tables were set up to display traditional clothing, vestments, artifacts and literature from churches around the globe. This area remained open during the "*encounter*" phase, in which participants could meet and listen to groups of Christians from other cultures elaborating on the particular challenges they face in expressing the gospel in ways appropriate to their own culture.

There were 27 such *encontros* introducing such varied contexts for Christian mission as the alienated youth culture of Germany, competition with Muslim evangelists in Africa, the "market-driven economies" of many industrialized nations and the desire of the indigenous Sami people of the Nordic countries to preserve their ancient culture while expressing their Christian faith.

Exploration of the conference theme began with a series of

onslaught in Russia as an "invasion by another culture" bent on remaking Russian culture "in the Western mode".

The heart of the exploration took place in the four inter-related sections into which participants were divided: "Authentic witness within each culture", "Gospel and identity in community", "Local congregations in pluralist societies" and "One gospel – diverse expressions". Drawing on preparatory materials for the conference and on discussions within the sections, four reports were drafted for discussion by the conference as a whole in the final two days.

As a way of expressing *engagement*, the delegates affirmed a number of "Acts of Commitment". They pledged to continue to explore ways of "addressing the tensions and divisions which arise when churches are confronted with the legitimate aspirations of the oppressed" and of "drawing out the gifts of the Spirit in all members of the body of Christ, so that they may fully participate in the total life and mission of the church".

For many participants, engagement was movingly expressed in the daily conference worship services. The most striking of these was the service held at Solar do Unhao, the site of the infamous dock in Salvador where for 300 years, beginning in 1550, men and women kidnapped in Africa landed as slaves in Brazil.

The participants walked in a guided meditation from the dock

The pulsating rhythms of Brazilian drummers called participants to the opening worship at the conference on world mission and evangelism.

addresses and panel discussions on mission, evangelism and the Bible.

The keynote speakers were Kenyan Lutheran theologian Musimbi Kanyoro and Russian Orthodox Metropolitan Kirill of Smolensk. Drawing on their own contexts, both pointed to human suffering and moral decay as the central challenges for those who proclaim the gospel. In Africa, Kanyoro said, human suffering is making "our times ripe for flirting with hopelessness"; Kirill lamented the "ecumenical disaster" of proselytism in his country, describing it as a "crusade against the Russian church" which has created a situation no less difficult than Communist rule. Both also referred to the oppressive face of culture. Kanyoro spoke of how "cultural imperatives" silence many African women while imposing harmful practices on them; Kirill described the mission

where the slave ships landed, past a white stucco shed where historians say the slaves were classified by age, gender, size and health, to a small church behind the dock where water was thrown on the slaves in a collective "baptism".

After the singing of an African American spiritual and a prayer of confession, WCC President Aaron Tolen of Cameroon reminded the worshippers that the guilt for the slave trade did not belong only to the Europeans who transported human beings as cargo across the Atlantic. "We Africans share in the responsibility," Tolen said. "We have degraded ourselves by selling our brothers and sisters as goods."

In a symbolic gesture, a brick from a fortress in Ghana where the slaves were loaded onto ships, which had been brought to the conference by Janice Nessibou of the Presbyterian Church in Ghana, was presented to the local Afro-Brazilian community.

Health, community and justice

Capacity-building – finding ways to enable people at the local level to address immediate everyday issues affecting their lives – has been a central focus of WCC endeavours to link the mission of the church with concerns for health, community and justice.

Within the WCC, CMC (Churches' Action for Health) and URM (Urban Rural Mission) are longstanding expressions of this dimension of ecumenical mission action and reflection.

CMC – the initials recall its earlier name "Christian Medical Commission" – marked its 25th anniversary in 1994. It grew out of the historical connection between foreign mission and health care, evident in medical mission – the earlier practice of building hospitals, clinics and dispensaries on the "mission field" and sending doctors and nurses along with evangelists and preachers.

Urban Rural Mission – a fusion of movements for Rural Mission and Urban Industrial Mission which emerged in the 1960s – has encouraged an understanding and practice of mission in which churches manifest solidarity with those who have been made poor and marginalized in their efforts to resist injustice.

The work of CMC, which is widely known through its bimonthly publication *Contact* (which appears in English, French, Spanish and Portuguese), centres on assisting a network of national church-related health coordinating agencies. Increasingly, the question facing these bodies is that of sustainability: how to meet increasing demands with diminishing resources.

A global consultation of these agencies in 1995 allowed for a broad exchange of information about how they approach their task as well as a discussion of the Christian values that motivate their work. An international directory has been published, giving information about the agencies.

Ongoing CMC work in this area involves regular visits to regional and national bodies for evaluation and advice.

The pressure on church health ministries in many contexts is growing as a result of economic "structural adjustment programmes", imposed on their government by international financial agencies. Government health services are often one of the first areas to be cut; and as a result more and more poor people are turning to church agencies asking for free health care. But the ecumenical partners who provide financial support for these agencies are finding it difficult to respond positively to rising requests.

On the agenda in nearly every CMC visit during this period has been an exploration of how churches can foster congregation-based health and healing activities which are preventative in nature and target specific groups of people at risk. One outcome of this has been the development of pilot programmes in youth-to-youth anti-substance abuse campaigns in a dozen churches in Ghana and an interdenominational group in Namibia.

A nurse in a crowded waiting room at a family health service centre in Gaza.

CMC's location in Geneva offers it an opportunity to maintain close contact with such bodies as the World Health Organization and the International Federation of Red Cross and Red Crescent Societies, drawing on the resources of these bodies and in turn contributing insights from the churches into their deliberations and programmes.

URM has sought over the past seven years to strengthen its regional focus, particularly by encouraging its regional networks to take greater responsibility for raising their own funds. At the same time, it has been working to highlight more clearly the specifically mission dimension of its engagement for social transformation: to encourage churches to be faithful in their mission to "the mission of God, which includes identification with people in pain and suffering, in their struggles for justice and in their resistance to structures of oppression, exclusion and exploitation".

A key event during this period was a global URM consultation in Seattle in August 1994. On the agenda was an evaluation of various methodologies of community organizing – the strategy for social transformation which it has always emphasized. Six stories of community organizing in different parts of the world highlighted both the range of approaches and the rich variety of ways in which communities of poor people are recognizing and making real the image of God in them.

Consultation participants heard about a Christian fellowship of rural and industrial labourers in Sri Lanka, migrant women garment workers in El Paso, Texas, traditional fishing communities in Chile, striking garbage collectors in Cairo, public housing estate residents in Melbourne and women organizing a community on the outskirts of Dakar, Senegal.

The last of these stories was an illustration that the struggles for justice in local communities which are at the heart of the URM vision may also include people of other faiths, for the community in question was predominantly Muslim.

The story which Khady N'Diaye told was about a group of poor families who had been relocated – "with the complicity of the World Bank and the government of Senegal" – from one part of the capital Dakar to a remote area near the sea without public services or transportation.

The initial impetus behind this community's decision to organize itself and address government neglect was a religious one: the insistence of the men that the first thing these families needed in their new location was a mosque:

"So they started to make bricks to build their mosque. As good wives, when we saw the trouble our husbands were having, we took it upon ourselves to lend a hand. So we went round to the markets asking for charity, and every time we got something we sold it for money, and we began to take over the building of the mosque."

From that small and unusual initiative grew a protracted and lively struggle, led chiefly by women, to improve the life of the community. In order to carry on that work, Khady N'Diaye told the WCC consultation, "we need support of course. *But we want it to start with ourselves and to be adapted to our situation.*"

That is an insight which lies behind all the WCC's efforts in capacity-building.

Education

The story is told of a young man who was seeking membership in the Communist Party of what used to be the Armenian Soviet Socialist Republic. When he emerged from his interview with local Party leaders, his waiting friends asked him how it had gone.

"With God's blessing I succeeded," he told them.

But if this anecdote illustrates how shallow the Communists' unrelenting efforts to promote atheism were, there is no denying that the restrictions imposed on the churches in this part of the world left them facing a formidable challenge once they regained the right openly to conduct religious education of their members.

This was a major ecumenical concern at the beginning of the 1990s; and at its first meeting in 1991, the WCC Central Committee mandated assistance to the churches of Central and Eastern Europe and the former Soviet Union, especially the Orthodox churches, in their educational work.

The specific goals identified for this programme laid out an ambitious agenda: building up the faith of the large number of people seeking baptism, strengthening local churches against missionary competition from abroad, recovering the Orthodox way of teaching the Christian faith, relating the content of Orthodox teaching to world problems, training religion teachers for churches and public schools, and – against the background of growing tension among the churches – promoting ecumenical collaboration in teacher-training.

As it developed over the next six years, the WCC programme focused on curriculum development, leadership training and training in course-writing. Several consultations were convened, workshops were organized, a month-long exposure visit to the USA was arranged for ten persons involved in religious education in Bulgaria, Romania, the Czech Republic and Russia, and a number of publications were released.

A key consultation was the Orthodox symposium on curriculum development hosted by Kykko Monastery in Cyprus in March 1994. In an intensive weeklong encounter, the participants identified and discussed ways of overcoming specific obstacles churches were facing as they sought to meet the needs for religious education in their context.

Among these were outdated textbooks and unqualified instructors of religion in public schools, increasingly chauvinistic, isolationist and fundamentalist attitudes among many people, leading them to identify ecumenism with proselytism

The Orthodox education centre at Vysoko-Petrovsky monastery, Moscow.

from abroad, the inadequacy of existing resources for church education programmes, which dated back to before the Communist revolution, the absence of pedagogically trained persons in the churches, and the general social and economic instability in most of these countries.

Despite these severe limitations, the churches were facing growing demands. More and more young people were being attracted to new Sunday Schools in nearly every parish, summer camps, flourishing catechetical centres, icon-painting schools and workshops, pilgrimages and choirs.

The participants agreed on a number of recommendations regarding the content, approach and methods of authentic Orthodox religious education. Fundamentally, they said, this should be seen as a lifelong process of bringing people to God through the church, building on the Bible and the liturgy as the pillars of the faith. It should integrate theology, history, lives of the saints, hymns, ethics and contemporary issues.

While recognizing the central role of the priest in the church community, the participants insisted that lay people, particularly those with pedagogical training, are essential partners in this enterprise. The content of the curriculum should be developmentally appropriate, encouraging creative and independent thinking, given the lack of such an emphasis in the educational systems of the past. Moreover, the Christian teaching of children cannot be confined to the classroom but must reach out to the parents as well.

The overall programme has benefited from active support by Orthodox churches around the world, in both hosting meetings and providing financial aid, as well as from the Lutheran Church in Finland. But although a number of meetings were held to further the goal of ecumenical teacher training, a major expansion of this aspect of the programme was discouraged by the ecumenical atmosphere in many of the churches, reflecting the tense situation mentioned earlier.

Under consideration now is the creation of an Inter-Orthodox Religious Education Centre to continue the work begun by the WCC in the period after 1998.

Besides addressing the particular needs of one part of the Council's membership, WCC education work over the past seven years has given continued attention to the challenges of Christian education in religiously and culturally pluralistic societies, including programmes on women and interfaith living and curriculum development in India, and to family life education.

HIV/AIDS: are churches responding to the challenge?

AIDS was first recognized in the USA in 1981 and detected in some African countries in 1982 (though subsequent research suggests that it was responsible for high fatality rates much earlier). The virus which causes it, now generally known as the Human Immuno-Deficiency Virus (HIV), was identified in 1983-84, though its origins remain unknown.

Since then HIV/AIDS has reached nearly every country in the world. What began as an *epidemic* (an infection or disease with and rapid and increasing rate of spread) is now *endemic* – entrenched and spreading steadily. More and more people worldwide are falling sick, suffering physically, emotionally and spiritually – many in abandonment and desolation. Men, women, young people and children are dying. Families and communities are severely affected socially and economically, particularly in less affluent countries. The effects of HIV/AIDS are impoverishing people, violating their human rights and wreaking havoc on their bodies and spirits.

Already in the 1980s, AIDS was on the agenda of the WCC, notably through the work of the Christian Medical Commission, which produced and distributed basic educational materials about it for health workers. In a statement in 1987, the WCC Executive Committee identified the heart of the issue for the churches: "The AIDS crisis challenges us profoundly to be the church in deed and in truth: *to be the church as a healing community*."

The spread of AIDS throughout the 1990s makes it evident that being such a healing community goes far beyond medical concerns. So, when the WCC Central Committee decided in 1994 to form a consultative group to conduct an ecumenical study on HIV/AIDS, it identified three areas of response: theology and ethics, pastoral care and the church as a healing community, and justice and human rights.

Members of the consultative group were chosen to reflect a diversity of experiences, geographical, cultural and confessional contexts and professional qualifications. Besides theologians, local pastors, pastoral counsellors and ethicists, there were virologists and physicians, specialists in human rights, and persons living with AIDS, directly affected by AIDS or working with AIDS-related movements. In December 1995, before the group had finished its work, one of its members, Brazilian Methodist lay theologian and liturgist Ernesto Cardoso, died as a result of an AIDS-related infection.

The work of the group was itself a kind of ecumenical journey. As its members listened to and learned from each other, tensions surfaced. Sensitive issues led to long deliberations. Sometimes members acknowledged having to rethink firmly held convictions in the light of what they heard. The end result was not complete unanimity: different members reached different conclusions on certain aspects of the study. But the report does speak of their achieving a high degree of unity and common vision in the face of seemingly irreconcilable positions.

The consultative group was keen not to produce a strictly analytical or academic report, far removed from the sufferings, struggles and joys of everyday life. So they complemented some of their meetings with exposure visits to AIDS-related projects and to individuals and communities living with HIV/AIDS in South Africa, the USA and India. Their report also drew on a long-term WCC participatory action research project on AIDS in East Africa and an international workshop in Vellore, India, on women and AIDS.

The report acknowledges that, with notable exceptions, the churches' record on AIDS has been inadequate. Indeed, sometimes churches have made the problem worse, whether through their silence, or by blocking open discussion, or even by reinforcing racist attitudes and neglect because AIDS has occurred predominantly among certain ethnic or racial groups.

In this sense, the report suggests, AIDS "has acted as a spotlight, exposing and revealing many iniquitous conditions in our personal and community lives which we have not been willing to confront. The pandemic reveals the tragic consequences of personal actions which directly harm others and of negligence which opens persons to additional risk."

Thus, AIDS challenges the churches "to be better informed, more active and more faithful witnesses to the gospel of reconciliation in their own lives and in their communities".

A statement based on the AIDS study was adopted by the WCC Central Committee in 1996 and commended to the churches. It surveys the impact of HIV/AIDS and identifies the various dimensions of the pandemic on which the consultative group focused: theological, ethical, human rights, pastoral care and counselling. It concludes with specific recommendations to churches, challenging them to confront both the immediate effects and causes of HIV/AIDS and the long-term factors which encourage its spread.

The Central Committee also asked that a longer report by the consultative group be published; and this study document appeared in 1997 under the title *Facing AIDS: The Challenge, The Churches' Response*. Scattered through it are excerpts from statements by church bodies, stories and personal narratives, case studies and scientific and United Nations reports.

In addition, the WCC produced a video on AIDS, drawing largely on work with persons living with AIDS in which the Church of Christ in Thailand has been closely involved.

An ecumenical workshop on communicating HIV/AIDS concerns in Chiang Mai, Thailand, offered opportunities to speak with people living with AIDS – as well as a pertinent reminder of all-too-common attitudes, also found in the church, towards these persons.

Programme to Overcome Violence

It was an historic moment when the WCC Central Committee met in Johannesburg, South Africa, in January 1994. Free elections, then a little over three months away, would mark the end of the apartheid era – and thus of an era in the life of the World Council as well.

Many of those assuming important roles in South Africa during this period of transition were church people who had worked closely with the WCC over the difficult years when it provided international leadership for the struggle of churches against this system of white minority domination. And the WCC's Programme to Combat Racism, which had been at the centre of this engagement, was marking the 25th anniversary of the consultation which had given birth to it in Notting Hill, London, in 1969.

But the euphoria in South Africa was tempered by anxiety about the violence and bloodshed in several parts of the country, which were threatening its hopes for a peaceful revolution.

Whatever the unique features of the violence in South Africa, it was clearly part of a worldwide phenomenon. And so, when Methodist Bishop Stanley Mogoba, the only church leader imprisoned on Robben Island during the apartheid years, called in his opening sermon for the WCC to follow the pattern of the Programme to Combat Racism and institute a Programme to Combat Violence, his words found an immediate resonance.

The discussion by the Central Committee unfolded a range of related concerns – among them domestic violence, urban violence, political violence, war and pacifism, violence rooted in ethnic tensions, the glorification of violence in the media, violence justified by the way churches read the Bible or do theology.

But there was overwhelming support for Bishop Mogoba's suggestion, though in response to the concerns of some that the word "combat" was inappropriate, it was agreed that the title of the new initiative should be the "Programme to Overcome Violence" (POV).

Its emphasis would be on practical ways of building a culture of peace by overcoming violence at different levels of society, encouraging the churches to take a lead in the use of appropriate nonviolent means, including prevention, mediation, intervention and education.

Mandated as a Council-wide programme, POV at first had difficulty finding a focus, precisely because its potential scope was so wide. And if no one could dispute the significance of the issue, discovering how to integrate this new initiative into existing priorities and activities was not easy.

In September 1996, drawing on a consultation in Rio de Janeiro earlier that year, the Central Committee approved a global campaign under the title "Peace to the City".

The intention of this campaign is not to examine urban violence as such – its realities and complexities are well-known – but to highlight constructive and imaginative bridge-building efforts already going on to overcome violence within specific communities touched by it.

Seven cities were eventually selected. They are located in all parts of the world: Belfast, Northern Ireland, in Europe; Boston in North America; Colombo, Sri Lanka, in Asia; Durban, in South Africa; Kingston, Jamaica, in the Caribbean; Rio de Janeiro, Brazil, in Latin America; and Suva, Fiji, in the Pacific.

The idea behind the campaign is that making visible creative models of community rebuilding by groups in the climate of violence in these cities can help others to see the value of some existing approaches to and methodologies for overcoming violence.

Sharing and networking among the groups in these seven cities is intended to express solidarity with and support for them. And telling their story more widely can give hope to concerned church-related groups in other communities that face similar problems and perhaps stimulate them to undertake similar endeavours of their own.

Stories from the seven cities, distributed through a variety of media, will give visibility to the programme and the efforts being undertaken. One early initiative has been the opening of a Peace to the City site on the WorldWideWeb for exchange of ideas and insights.

In addition, the Programme to Overcome Violence has opened up new lines of collaboration between the WCC and the Historic Peace Churches – churches coming from the so-called "Radical Reformation" tradition, including Mennonites, Brethren and Quakers – for whom the rejection of war and violence and the advocacy of ministries of peace have been a central identifying mark. Some of these churches are members of the WCC, but many have remained outside of formal ecumenical fellowship; and their involvement in this new WCC initiative is an enrichment for the Council and the ecumenical movement.

Justice, Peace and Creation

WCC work in the areas defined in the title of the unit on Justice, Peace and Creation has included diverse activities historically rooted in the Life and Work tradition, as well as issues related to women and young people in church and society.

Liberia: war and violence are a way of life in many parts of the world.

Theology of life: seeking the local-global links

One legacy of the Life and Work movement, which began with a world conference in Stockholm in 1925 and merged with Faith and Order to form the WCC in 1948, has been a developing tradition of ecumenical social thought.

Over the years, a succession of central themes have reflected the changing world in which the churches seek to witness. There was the search for a "responsible society" in the face of the human "disorder" of which the theme of the Amsterdam assembly spoke. Later, this gave way to examination of the churches' role in the "rapid social change" that accompanied the end of the colonial era. In the 1970s, the quest was for a "just, participatory and sustainable society", as the persistence of poverty and misery and the limits of and threats to the earth's capacity to sustain human life became ever more clearly recognized.

Between the WCC's sixth (Vancouver) and seventh (Canberra) assemblies, the rallying point was the appeal to undertake common action on issues of justice, peace and the integrity of creation (JPIC) as part of the essence of what it means to be the church. While the heart of the JPIC process itself was the call to the churches to make public commitments to confront the threats to life in these areas, it was accompanied by renewed ecumenical ethical reflection as well.

Since Canberra, this effort has centred on articulating a "theology of life". The link between this and the JPIC process is the ten affirmations made by the 1990 world convocation on JPIC:

– all exercise of power is accountable to God;
– God's option for the poor;
– the equal value of all races and peoples;
– male and female are created in the image of God;
– truth is at the foundation of a community of free people;
– the peace of Jesus Christ;
– the creation as beloved of God;
– the earth is the Lord's;
– the dignity and commitment of the younger generation;
– human rights are given by God.

The heart of the theology of life programme was a series of 22 case studies by local groups from around the world. Each group examined one of the ten affirmations and sought to understand both what it implied in its own context and how these local elements fit into a global analysis.

The reports of these case studies were presented at what was surely one of the most unusual meetings ever of a WCC advisory body: the January 1997 meeting of the commission for the unit on Justice, Peace and Creation, held near Nairobi. The gathering took the form of a *sokoni*, which is the Swahili word for "marketplace". But while a certain amount of commerce took place in this market – sales of banners and quilts, posters and cards, photographs and artworks – its energy came from the wider reality of the *sokoni* as a place where people come to meet others and to exchange not only goods but also information and ideas.

The commission members and staff were joined each day by local visitors – church leaders, development workers and government officials, as well as women's and youth groups, drummers, musicians and church choirs, artists and actors, farmers, workers and traders, refugees, widows and orphans.

On the training grounds of the Kenya Commercial Bank, the Kenyan hosts had built seven huts, whose design and structure reflected traditional African cosmology. The 22 case studies were clustered into six themes and each was assigned a hut.

Participants moved from hut to hut according to their interests, talking and listening, telling stories, buying handicrafts by local artisans. The women's hut offered a continuous participatory quilting session. One participant set up a chair where he shined shoes for anyone who was willing to talk to him while he was doing the polishing. Each day began with drumbeats, sometimes accompanied by a flute, and ended with a *lala salama* (Swahili for "good night") around a bonfire where participants shared their experiences, insights and reflections from the day, then danced or listened to stories told by Kenyan poet Bantu Mwaura.

The style of presenting the case studies varied as much as the studies themselves: stories, poetry, drama, role-playing, panels, singing and dancing. A poignant symbol was a scroll carried in procession from hut to hut, on which were written the names of those from different countries who have given their lives to struggles for justice, peace and creation.

Participants identified a number of elements which contributed to the success of the *sokoni*. Some highlighted the diversity of experiences shared by people living out the same commitments in very different settings. Others pointed to the open space in which this sharing took place. And many noted the predominance of the oral tradition: never before had documents played so small a role in a meeting of the WCC. All agreed on the importance of involving local people, not just for formal greetings and logistical support but as part of the process, witnessing to their own faith by telling their own stories of pain and suffering, struggle and hope.

In his address welcoming the participants, WCC general secretary Konrad Raiser insisted that this local emphasis was not just a matter of convenience but reflected a conviction that the ecumenical ministry of the WCC should begin not with global analyses but by "listening to the voice and experience of people in local situations and then trying to organize the exchange, the mutual questioning, the learning, the fresh discoveries and also new questions".

Economics and Christian faith

Through the Life and Work movement, dedicated to working for church unity through collaboration in social action and social justice, economics came onto the ecumenical agenda at an early stage.

Not long after the 1925 Stockholm conference which launched the Life and Work movement came the worldwide economic depression of the 1930s. Massive unemployment and inflation created the climate for political upheaval, especially in Europe; and for a time the Life and Work movement employed an economist to help the churches to think through the consequences of these issues for their witness in the world.

Economics has been a WCC concern over the years. A key emphasis of the Programme to Combat Racism, for example, was the economic roots of racism.

During the 1980s a useful instrument for WCC endeavours in this area was the Advisory Group on Economic Matters, through which the Council drew on professional economists to produce a series of studies on how major topics in contemporary economics bear on the concerns of the churches and the ecumenical movement.

A growing ecumenical preoccupation at that time was the massive external debt burdening many countries in the South and the consequences of this for the poorest and most vulnerable people in those societies. WCC studies looked at how international financial organizations such as the World Bank and International Monetary Fund operate.

The relationship between Christian faith and economic issues was given a high profile by the publication of a pastoral letter on the subject by the Roman Catholic bishops in the United States, which drew on the long tradition of Roman Catholic social thought. Some suggested that a similarly comprehensive text on the relevance of contemporary economic issues to the church and its mission might come from the WCC. To be sure, the difference between the World Council as a fellowship of churches and the Roman Catholic Church as a single church with a central authority structure would mean that a WCC document of this type would have quite a different status. Yet it could nevertheless serve a useful function in bringing together insights from within the Council's member churches in their diverse contexts around the world.

A process towards an eventual ecumenical statement on economic life was mandated by the WCC Central Committee in

A street scene in Beijing: fashions, automobiles and fast-food chains are all part of a global economy.

1988. An international and interconfessional group of economists, social scientists, politicians, ethicists and theologians was convened, and an intensive process of regional meetings, consultations on specific topics and solicitation of reactions and input from member churches was set in motion.

In the end, the Central Committee received the text on *Christian Faith and the World Economy Today* as a study document to be commended to the member churches. In addition to the WCC's working languages – English, French, German, Russian and Spanish – it has subsequently been translated into Arabic, Chinese, Danish, Greek and Portuguese.

The process leading to the drafting of the final document, which has served as the framework for much of the WCC's work on economic issues in the 1990s, made a special effort to incorporate reflection on Christian faith and economics by Christian economists outside the membership of the WCC, as well as to involve economists, ethicists and theologians from Orthodox churches. Among the meetings held to discuss the report were a consultation in Jordan, co-sponsored with the Middle East Council of Churches; a seminar for young theological lecturers from Eastern and Central Europe to explore how economic issues might be included in the curriculum of theological education; and a consultation in Moscow in September 1994 on "Economy, Values and Society in Russia".

However, in March 1997 plans to organize with the Amity Foundation and two other local partners a consultation in Beijing on "Socialism and the Market Economy" –

which would have focused on China's experiment with a socialist market economy and the experience of countries in transition – had to be called off at the last minute when the Communist Party withdrew its authorization. It is hoped that this consultation can be rescheduled at a later date.

While the WCC study document only touches on some topics which clearly need deeper ecumenical exploration, the Council has also been involved in a collaborative venture with the Visser 't Hooft Foundation and the Ecumenical Institute in Bossey which has organized three consultations to take up some of these issues.

The participants in these consultations, all of which have centred on the notion of "sustainability", have come from a variety of backgrounds: not only churches and ecumenical partners, but also the academic world, UN-related organizations, trade unions and business.

Materials from the three consultations – "Sustainable Growth: A Contradiction in Terms?", "Work in a Sustainable Society", and "Globalization and Sustainability" – have been published as articles and booklets and in the WCC's quarterly journal *The Ecumenical Review.*

Accelerated climate change

"Talking about the weather" has taken on a new meaning as public awareness has grown of changes in the global climate, the extent to which these may be caused by human activity and their potentially serious consequences for the habitability of certain parts of the world and the sustainability of human life.

While WCC work on climate change in the 1990s has largely focused on the tortuous process towards international agreements on reducing carbon dioxide emissions through diminished dependency on fossil fuels, the issue was already on its agenda prior to the Earth Summit in Rio de Janeiro in 1992, which inaugurated this intergovernmental process.

The world convocation on Justice, Peace and the Integrity of Creation in Seoul in 1989 selected global warming as the focal point of its attention to threats to the integrity of creation and called on the churches to covenant together to address this. Already at Seoul, the churches' special role in encouraging and exemplifying needed changes in life-style was underscored.

Later, the term "global warming" has been replaced by "accelerated climate change" to emphasize the wider implications of the projected rises in average global temperature due to human activity, including greater irregularity and unpredictability of the weather and more violent storms.

The WCC has monitored the intergovernmental negotiations on climate change since work on a UN Framework Convention on Climate Change began immediately after the Earth Summit in 1992; and WCC-related teams have been present at the major intergovernmental meetings on the subject.

A task group on climate change prepared an initial draft of a study document, which was then discussed at regional consultations in Africa, South Asia, Europe and North America, and revised at an international consultation in Driebergen, the Netherlands, in October 1993.

The Central Committee commended this text – *Accelerated Climate Change: Sign of Peril, Test of Faith* – to the churches in January 1994. Subsequently translated into seven languages, it has been widely circulated not only among churches but also to governments and international and non-governmental organizations.

To enrich the ecumenical input into the international discussion, the specific effects of climate change and other environmental threats for different parts of the world were investigated in cooperation with regional ecumenical organizations in Africa, Asia, Latin America and the Pacific; and papers from a second consultation in Driebergen, this one focusing on "Climate Change and Just and Sustainable Communities", were published in *The Ecumenical Review*. In the context of the international negotiations, the WCC advocated the special concerns of a group of low-lying "small-island states", mostly in the South Pacific, which are threatened with catastrophe, even total disappearance, if warmer ocean waters lead to rising sea levels.

Another consultation, this one at the Ecumenical Academy in Bad Boll, Germany, explored mobility – the environmental effects of rapidly growing international travel – which has become a major issue emerging from the climate change discussion.

To engage churches in its efforts, the WCC organized a petition campaign aimed at encouraging churches in industrialized countries to press their governments to follow through on commitments to reduce carbon dioxide emissions. The petitions, distributed widely (including through the WCC site on the WorldWideWeb), were presented to government officials at a meeting in Bonn in April 1997.

An important side-effect of the Climate Change programme and its various consultations and activities has been the development of a growing network of persons responsible for environmental concerns within WCC member churches.

Besides its substantive contributions to the climate change debate, this programme has been widely hailed as a model for other areas of future WCC staff work. Coordination of the programme has been the responsibility of David Hallman, who has devoted part of his time to the WCC while remaining on the staff of the United Church of Canada. Much of the coordinating work has thus been done in Toronto rather than Geneva.

The WCC and Africa
a framework for solidarity and engagement

"Many experts and observers of the African situation have concluded that Africa is a hopeless case that might as well be written off by the rest of the world. They have painted a bleak future for Africa. We refuse to accept such a conclusion... We commit ourselves to work selflessly towards the realization of a different and better future for Africa, a future of life in abundance."

That pledge was made by some 80 people from all parts of Africa attending a May 1997 conference organized by the WCC. The conference culminated a two-year programme of study and dialogue on Reconstructing Africa. Its venue in Johannesburg and its theme, "Jubilee and the African Kairos", pointed to two significant elements of the WCC's involvement in Africa through the 1990s.

At the beginning of the decade, holding a WCC meeting in South Africa would have been unthinkable. The end of the apartheid system in 1994 not only posed new challenges for South African churches but also signalled a new phase of international ecumenical engagement in the country.

The conference theme encompassed the hopes for a new beginning inherent in the biblical jubilee, with its connotations of restoration, liberation and reconciliation, and the urgency linked with the concept of "kairos", a special moment of God's grace. "Jubilee" was given further significance by the plans to celebrate the WCC's own jubilee – its 50th anniversary – at its eighth assembly in Harare in 1998. And "kairos" had been an important rallying-point for Christian involvement in the struggle against apartheid, subsequently picked up by many groups in other parts of the world.

The immediate antecedents of the Reconstructing Africa initiative were in the Ecumenical Monitoring Programme in South Africa, through which the WCC had coordinated the sending of international church observers to South Africa during the process of transition to a democratic government. Once elections had taken place in April 1994, the decision was made to extend the scope of ecumenical monitoring activities to other parts of Africa where the search for democracy was being affected by political violence.

In fact, the WCC sought throughout the 1990s to develop an overall framework for ecumenical solidarity and engagement with the people of this continent where the church is growing more quickly than anywhere else. Such a unified approach to Africa was meant not only to coordinate activities undertaken by the WCC and its ecumenical partners in Africa but also to stimulate a new way of looking at Africa, a new vision holding up life, justice and peace, and human dignity. The desire to affirm such a vision was an important factor in the decision to hold the eighth assembly in Africa.

Crises in many individual African countries were often on the agenda of the WCC during the decade. In addition to standing beside churches during epochal changes in Namibia, South Africa, Angola, Mozambique and Malawi, international, regional and national ecumenical bodies sought ways to confront the horror of mass killings in Rwanda and to avert the outbreak of bloodshed on the same scale elsewhere in the Great Lakes region. The suffering of millions in the interminable civil strife in Sudan, coups and civil war in Liberia and Sierra Leone, the overthrow of Mobutu Sese Seko in Zaïre (now the Democratic Republic of Congo), the repeated delays in restoring civilian rule in Nigeria and the ongoing oppression of the Ogoni people – all attracted particular attention from the WCC.

While situations such as these certainly lent a sense of urgency to the Reconstructing Africa programme, one of its overriding concerns was to transcend responses of fatalism and despair which write off Africa as a hopeless case or portray it only as a helpless victim of exploitation from outside. And a primary emphasis to emerge was insistence that the leadership in this search must come from Africans.

A series of solidarity visits around the continent revealed common threads to the situation in many places. Chief among these is the compelling need for unity in the face of the fragmenting and dehumanizing effects of a "culture of survival and violence", which also affects the churches, many of which operate more and more like competitive private enterprises.

Yet the primary tones of the Reconstructing Africa report are hopeful ones. On the basis of the ecumenical exchange visits in various regions, the report says that "a new pan-African spirit is emerging. Africans of all walks of life, ages and classes have been questioning the status quo, and struggling to understand the reasons behind the prevailing situation of war, conflict and economic instability."

Against this background, the study process linked with the programme offered tools for analysis and mobilization to representatives of all parts of society – religious and political leaders, academics and students, women and young people, trade unionists and business people. Four chief areas of study were identified: *faith and politics*, emphasizing democracy and good governance; *faith and economics*, concentrating on land, labour and capital; *mission and culture*, focusing on communication, human dignity and national identity; and *ecumenism and civil society*, addressing the churches' ambivalence about partnership with governments and other organizations seeking to meet human needs.

Participants in the jubilee conference insisted that the church should neither alienate itself from government nor become a tool of the governing groups. What is needed is "a new partnership with African society and the state, maintaining a critical solidarity in all that is just. The African church, true to its vocation, should guard the rights of the powerless, the vulnerable and the poor."

Leaving the conference, they articulated an African jubilee vision for the new millennium: "a vision that calls us to work together and creatively... to eliminate the barriers and walls that divide and

enslave us, to reconcile broken relationships and heal the wounds inflicted by violent ways of resolving conflict...; a vision that can be realized if Africans agree to work together in the spirit of pan-Africanism and manage their human and natural resources responsibly and ethically."

A village school in the north of Malawi.

In Ethiopia, where there is a shortage of firewood, cow dung is dried so that it can be used as fuel.

A small village on the Upper Nile, Sudan.

Human rights

Two years before the World Council of Churches was officially founded in Amsterdam in 1948, the WCC in process of formation joined with the International Missionary Council to establish the Commission of the Churches on International Affairs (CCIA).

Among the earliest concerns of the ecumenical movement was religious liberty; and CCIA was instrumental in the formulation of Article 18 in the Universal Declaration of Human Rights, which guarantees this freedom. Over the years since then, promoting human rights and defending those whose human rights are being violated have continued to be among the WCC's priority concerns.

Carrying out this work ecumenically involves building contacts on the one hand with churches, ecumenical organizations and human rights bodies at the national and regional levels, and on the other hand with international human rights organizations and intergovernmental instruments like the United Nations Commission on Human Rights (which meets annually in Geneva) and its Centre for Human Rights.

Sometimes the Council acts in defence of human rights through pastoral or investigative missions to areas where extensive violations are being reported. On a more sustained basis, the WCC coordinates the participation of churches and related groups in providing testimony to UN bodies regarding human rights. Over the years the churches have established a solid reputation in this arena for the breadth and reliability of the information they – often uniquely – provide.

Behind these interventions in specific situations lies the continuous ecumenical monitoring of the global human rights situation. The accompanying analysis has enabled the WCC to build up an understanding of issues in the area of human rights which served as the background for its participation in the UN's world conference on human rights in Vienna in June 1995.

Since the Canberra assembly the Council has also conducted a global review of ecumenical policy and practice in human rights, carried out through regional meetings in all parts of the world. One new and important issue which surfaced during this review, particularly as a result of ecumenical engagement in defending human rights in Latin America, is impunity – the situation in which those accused of gross and systematic human rights violations or crimes against humanity are not charged, tried or punished, whether because of an

A meeting of members of the Ponca Nation, Oklahoma, during the WCC-sponsored team visit to the USA in 1994 to investigate racism as a violation of human rights.

amnesty or pardon or by deliberate inaction.

The Council was intensively engaged in human rights struggles in Latin America during the 1970s, when there was not yet a regional ecumenical organization there. In no fewer than 19 countries in Central and South America and the Caribbean, repressive military dictatorships used detention without trial, torture and "disappearances" as key instruments of their grip on power. As these countries have returned to civilian democracy, the question has arisen of how to deal with this period of their history and with those who were responsible for the repression. Similar questions have come up following the breakup of the former Yugoslavia, the end of apartheid in South Africa and the bloody ethnic strife in Rwanda.

On the one side are those who argue for reconciliation by way of amnesty and pardon, putting the past behind; on the other are those who insist that reconciliation with impunity – without requiring accountability from those who perpetrated crimes against their own fellow-citizens – would be a travesty of justice and no reconciliation at all.

In 1996 the WCC published a book on impunity, featuring case studies and reflections from ethical, legal and psychological perspectives drawn from six Latin American countries. Edited by Charles Harper, who had been in charge of what was then the WCC's Human Rights Resources Office for Latin America, the book has been widely hailed for insights whose implications for proclaiming a gospel of reconciliation extend far beyond that region.

Human rights served as the point of departure for an important WCC initiative

in the struggle against racism: a series of hearings, conducted by an international ecumenical team in the United States, which sought to establish an understanding of racism as something that violates human rights, and not just as an issue of civil rights.

The enduring issue of religious liberty, construed in the early years of the WCC largely in terms of the right of minority Christian churches to organize and worship according to their convictions, has reappeared on the ecumenical agenda. Despite the fact that freedom of religion is enshrined in the constitutions of most countries around the world, minority religious communities in many places in fact suffer from discrimination, oppression and even violence.

And, as a WCC consultation on religious liberty observed, new and deeper reflection is needed, also among the churches, on the subject of constitutional provisions regarding church-state relations, especially in countries and societies going through transition.

Throughout the 1990s, this issue has surfaced in many countries where religious liberty was seriously infringed during the period of the cold war, especially in some countries of Eastern and Central Europe and the former Soviet Union. In many places, the lifting of restrictions on religious activity has led to an influx of missionary groups from abroad. That in turn has created pressure for new legislation to restrict these activities. Many observers believe that the laws being drafted infringe on guarantees of religious freedom enshrined in the constitutions of these countries and the Universal Declaration of Human Rights.

Living letters
encouraging the churches' solidarity with women

The Ecumenical Decade – Churches in Solidarity with Women was launched by churches around the world during the Easter season in 1988. In January of the previous year, the WCC Central Committee had called for such a Decade following an assessment of the limited impact on the churches of the United Nations Decade for Women (1975-1985).

The Decade identified five areas of emphasis: empowering women to challenge oppressive structures; affirming their contributions to their churches and communities; giving visibility to their engagement in struggles for justice, peace and the integrity of creation; enabling churches to free themselves from racism, sexism, classism and discrimination; and encouraging church action in solidarity with women.

How churches took up the Decade and these concerns was to be determined locally, nationally and regionally. The Decade was not a centralized WCC programme but a framework for holding together common issues evident around the world. The Council's role was one of encouragement and support – monitoring and publicizing what was going on in various places, identifying emerging issues and insights, and building a network among those committed to the objectives of the Decade.

As the midpoint of the Decade approached, it was evident that it had indeed generated much enthusiasm which had taken shape in many creative initiatives around the world. Yet the solidarity of the *churches* with women was less apparent than the growing solidarity of women with other women and with the churches. So, an international gathering of women to evaluate the Decade in 1992 suggested that it had to be "offered back to the churches". The best way to do so, they said, was to go directly to each of the WCC's member churches through an organized programme of team visits.

While official, pastoral and fact-finding visits have long been a staple of ecumenical fellowship, never before had the WCC undertaken so extensive an initiative for first-hand encounter with its member churches. Although it did not prove possible to visit every church, by the time the programme ended in October 1996, the large majority of the 330 churches on the WCC's membership rolls had received a team – usually two men and two women, accompanied by a WCC staff member, with at least one of the members being a woman from the country or region visited.

Typically, the teams met with church leaders, with women's groups and movements, with members of congregations and ministers, with professors and students in schools of theology. The agenda varied according to the place; and the programmes were prepared by the churches visited. But all included conversations on four topics which had emerged as priorities during the Decade:
– violence against women in all its forms;
– women's participation in the life of the church;
– the particular effects on women of the global economic crisis;

– the impact of racism and xenophobia on women.

The purpose was not to evaluate the churches visited nor to conduct a scientific study of the status of women today. In line with the theme of the Decade itself, the visits were a way of expressing solidarity with women and encouraging the churches to move forward in their own commitments.

Each of the 75 teams wrote a report of what it had seen and heard, which was then forwarded to the receiving churches. While the reports themselves were not meant for publication, an international group of six women and one man read through them all – some 1500 pages – and prepared an extensive summary highlighting issues that surfaced most often during the course of the visits. This was published by the WCC in 1997 under the title *Living Letters* – drawing on an image from Paul's letter to the Corinthians.

In summing up the impact of the Decade and the visits, the group of readers noted that the capacity of the Decade to empower communities, women's groups and individuals was consistently evident. Some of the visits brought together groups within a church who had never before sat around the same table to reflect together about the concerns expressed in the Decade. Some prompted church leaders to discuss their solidarity with women for the first time.

Nevertheless, in some places the Decade had brought tensions among women and women's groups to the surface. The reports also made it clear that the Decade had not elicited the same kind of response from men as from women. Some men told the visiting teams that their church has more pressing priorities, or that the time is not ripe for "sweeping change" in their churches, or that the Decade's goals are too conflictual and would damage relations within the church, or with other churches, or with other faith communities, or with secular society or with the state. In a few places, resistance to the Decade and its objectives was framed in terms of the argument that these reflected the imposition of feminist concerns on other parts of the world by the West.

The Decade as such will conclude with an international festival in Harare in December 1998, just before the WCC assembly. But the reports and testimonies from those who took part in the Decade team visits – the visitors and visited alike – suggest that transforming churches into truly inclusive communities will be a continuing priority of the WCC into the new millennium.

A women's meeting in Geneva during the Ecumenical Decade, 1995.

Indigenous Peoples

The situation of Indigenous Peoples around the world has been a longstanding item on the ecumenical agenda. While the major focus of the Programme to Combat Racism for many years was on Southern Africa, its work also included the concerns, especially in the area of land rights, of Indigenous Peoples in the Americas, Aotearoa New Zealand and Australia.

That commitment was symbolized in the totem pole carved by Native Canadians and presented to the WCC at the sixth assembly in Vancouver in 1983; and it received further emphasis in the presence of the Aboriginal people of Australia at the seventh assembly in Canberra, which adopted a substantial declaration on "Land and Indigenous Peoples: Move Beyond Words".

For several reasons, the period since the Canberra assembly has seen a greater WCC involvement in this area. A major impetus came with the 500th anniversary in 1992 of the voyage of Christopher Columbus and a growing recognition among the churches of the genocidal consequences of the European "discovery" and subsequent colonization of the Americas for the peoples who had lived there for thousands of years.

At the same time, growing ecumenical concern with the integrity of creation recognized the challenges which indigenous spirituality poses to the dominant and destructive Western attitude towards creation.

And the concerns of Indigenous Peoples received greater international attention through the United Nations Year of Indigenous Peoples and the awarding of the 1992 Nobel Peace Prize to the Guatemalan Indigenous leader Rigoberta Menchú Tum.

To make the WCC's engagement in this area more effective, a consultant on indigenous issues was appointed for four years. Among the priorities identified were indigenous spirituality, land rights, advocacy for social justice and sharing of resources.

The topic of indigenous spirituality was addressed through a number of small consultations in Asia, South and Central America and Europe. These examined specifically how insights from these various contexts bear on the issue of expressing the one gospel in many cultures – thus becoming part of the process leading up to the WCC's world conference on mission and evangelism in 1996.

Aggravating threats to the land rights of Indigenous Peoples in many places are new technologies which make it possible to exploit again already-exploited mineral sources and to use great expanses of previously uncultivated land for agriculture. The WCC has given particular attention to land rights struggles of the Wichi and Mapuche peoples in Argentina, the Huicholes in Mexico, the Quechua in Peru and peoples in the Philippines.

Nobel Peace Prize winner Rigoberta Menchú Tum during her visit to WCC offices in Geneva in 1992.

The WCC took part in a global consultation on mining in London in 1996 which responded to growing concern among indigenous communities (forty of which were represented at the meeting) over severe damage to the land, water and air caused by mineral extraction. Out of that consultation was established a Global Information Network to share developments in this area.

Internationally, the WCC's involvement has also taken the form of support for indigenous groups taking part in United Nations forums, with a view to the drafting of an international declaration on the rights of Indigenous Peoples. These have included the UN Working Group on Indigenous Peoples and the UN Commission on Human Rights.

A related area of WCC concern and activity has been the liberation and identity of the millions of Dalit people in India – those who have been the victims of systematic exclusion and oppression because they were born outside the traditional Hindu caste structure, despite constitutional and legal provisions to alleviate this situation.

With the support of the WCC, the Dalit Solidarity Programme has grown up, bringing together Dalits in the Christian, Sikh, Buddhist, Muslim and Hindu communities. The WCC's specific role has been in raising financial support and in giving international visibility to the situation of the Dalits, including through the publication in 1997 of a book in its Risk series, *Downtrodden*.

Civil society and globalization

"Globalization" and "civil society" were two terms heard often in ecumenical discussions during the 1990s.

Neither term was entirely new. And both were used in so many different senses that their usefulness was sometimes called into question.

Yet despite the ambiguities, each term has in its way served as a focal point for significant reflection on the contemporary task of the church. Globalization offers a vision of "one world" quite different from that advanced by the ecumenical movement; and the civil society discussion has raised questions about how churches see themselves functioning alongside other groups and organizations at all levels in society, from the local to the international.

Awareness of the phenomenon of globalization grew after the fall of the Berlin Wall and the much-celebrated "triumph of the free market".

Rapid developments in technology and a growing insistence on expanding international trade have made possible massive concentrations of economic, financial and media power. This consolidation of the power of the already-powerful has widened the gaps between rich nations and poor nations and between the rich and the poor in nearly every nation. In some parts of the South, exploitation by the wealthy nations has given way to the reality of being completely disregarded and treated as "expendable" in the global system.

These developments have posed new challenges to the people's movements in various parts of the world with whom the WCC has over the years developed a network committed to action and reflection on issues of justice, and who have provided much of the energy for ecumenical social thought.

A lively discussion has grown up around the question of the role of "civil society" in a world dominated by political and, increasingly, economic powers. The subject of civil society and its implications for the life and work of the church and the ecumenical movement was the theme of an issue of *The Ecumenical Review*.

While this discussion has affirmed the role of the WCC in building international linkages of solidarity and partnership, much of the Council's programme on Civil Society and Life in Community was carried out in a decentralized manner, drawing especially on four major partners in Germany, Korea, the USA and South Africa.

In its first phase, the programme concentrated on disseminating ideas and experiences – both by conducting academic study and research into key issues, writing articles for existing publications and exchanging experiences across borders during local events and activities planned and organized by local partners.

Initiatives in involving churches at the local level in building democracy, resolving conflict and creating economic alternatives were a major thrust of the programme. Special emphasis was given to initiatives in South Africa, East Africa, Central and Eastern Europe and Cuba.

The civil society programme also collaborated with several other parts of the WCC in an assessment of local educational experiences and in organizing a major consulta-

Representatives of farmworkers' unions in Phoenix, Arizona, discuss the problem of Mexican migrants without documents crossing into the USA to find jobs in agriculture.

tion in Geneva on "Education for Empowerment, Education for Citizenship".

A consultation in Seoul in 1997 put forward the idea of using contemporary communication technologies to create a global network which would link together already-existing communication centres in a way that would promote much wider sharing of information about and insights into the engagement of faith communities in

concerns of justice, peace and creation.

The civil society programme has clearly surfaced some new approaches to the understanding of the role in society of the church and the ecumenical movement. Some work has been done on the theological implications of the civil society discussion for an understanding of the church and its mission, though it is evident that deeper reflection in this area is needed.

MENDES 1993
Ecumenical Global Gathering of Youth and Students

The Ecumenical Global Gathering of Youth and Students (EGGYS), which brought more than 500 young Christians to Mendes, Brazil, for ten days in July 1993, was the first such world youth meeting organized by the WCC in more than 40 years.

Earlier world Christian youth assemblies – in Amsterdam in 1939, Oslo in 1947 and Kottayam, India, in 1952 – were attended by representatives of only Protestant and Orthodox organizations. In Mendes, two Roman Catholic student organizations were among the organizers, along with the WCC, World Student Christian Federation, the world bodies for the YMCA and YWCA and international youth movements from the Lutheran, Orthodox and Reformed churches.

The participants' intensive quest for an ecumenical vision for the 21st century made it clear that feminism and contextual interpretation of the gospel are two of the most vital issues for the next ecumenical generation.

Violence, exploitation and repression against women – at home, at work and in the church – were concerns repeatedly expressed. Despite resistance in some quarters, many young women present spoke of their determination to change things.

Korean theologian Chung Hyun-Kyung, whose presentation at the WCC's seventh assembly in Canberra in 1991 had drawn passionate reactions both pro and con, was a keynote speaker at EGGYS. While the "Asian feminist liberation theology" about which she spoke was unacceptable to some participants, it was evident that most of the young people present felt keenly the alienation and hopelessness with which Chung's presentation grappled.

The participants themselves described varied experiences of fragmentation in their own contexts: racism and violence in South Africa, torture and disappearances in Chile, ethnic discrimination and linguistic problems in Canada, xenophobia in Europe, destruction and the separation of families in Lebanon, ethnic war in Sri Lanka, tensions between Catholics and Protestants in Colombia, deterioration of the social fabric in Brazil because of external debt. Women's struggles, religious fundamentalism, racism, ethnocentrism and social classes were identified as universal causes of fragmentation.

While seeking unity, EGGYS recognized the richness of human diversity. "Unity does not try to homogenize," said the report of one of the forums through which delegates expressed and synthesized

A dramatic exhibition of domestic animals and human garbage offered an unusual introduction to a Bible study session at the ecumenical youth gathering.

but no clear alternative vision; and the report ends by saying: "Our being conscious of this economic order is the foundation that will construct and guide our search for developing alternative models of economic action in our communities, churches and organizations."

Activism was not entirely absent. Participants in the forum on environment and development walked to the picturesque little town of Mendes, half an hour away, where they dredged garbage from the river, which provides water to Rio de Janeiro, and planted trees along its bank.

For many participants, EGGYS was their first trip outside their own country; and for the great majority it was their first international conference. The informal exchanges and friendships which developed were at least as important as the documents that emerged. The exchange of the peace during worship often extended to ten minutes, as hundreds roamed around seeking friends, embracing and kissing. And even the shy and awkward were drawn into the community dancing which concluded the Asia-Pacific and Latin American evening cultural programmes.

Apart from the network of personal bonds and relationships, EGGYS held out the promise of far closer cooperation among the organizations represented. Some urged that a global coordinating body be formed, but regional and national coordination were stressed far more. For predominantly Protestant and Orthodox organizations, EGGYS provided an opening to forge links with Roman Catholic youth organizations.

While some critical responses came in a joint "reflection" from Orthodox participants, the dominant note at EGGYS was the accommodation of differences. The main quest was for ways in which the world could live together in all its rich and sometimes contradictory diversity.

"We did not come with ready-made solutions but we came with a strong desire to share experiences and to work together," said a letter drafted on behalf of EGGYS participants to young people and participating churches, movements and organizations. In some ways EGGYS was itself a living exhibition of the achievements of ecumenism. Most of the young people present did not seem conscious of being from one Christian tradition or another. The thread running through all the forum discussions was rather concern for the weak and the marginalized. Balance was the hallmark of the gathering; indeed, there were more women present than men, and no nation, region or denomination dominated EGGYS.

their concerns. "Unfortunately, it is often the case that unity becomes manipulated in an attempt to draw the masses into a climate of passivity and dependence."

Besides unity in a fragmented world, other forums addressed the rights of people and democracy; women; economy, society and alternative models; environment and development; and education for life.

Indigenous Peoples' concerns were prominently expressed in the forum on the rights of people and democracy. The problems of Central and Eastern Europe featured both in that forum and in the one on economy, society and alternative models. The latter was perhaps the most difficult subject for participants to come to grips with. There was agreement on the inadequacies of the current structures,

WCC presence at United Nations world conferences

The period between the Canberra and Harare assemblies has been notable for a number of large and highly publicized United Nations world conferences. The WCC was especially involved in five of these, using its status as a nongovernmental organization (NGO) accredited to the UN's Economic and Social Council to offer a channel for participation by churches and ecumenical bodies and groups from around the world.

Of the five, the one which no doubt had the highest profile was the **Earth Summit** – the United Nations Conference on Environment and Development (UNCED), held in Rio de Janeiro in June 1992. As part of the preparatory process for UNCED, the WCC convened a series of meetings to provide contributions from faith communities for the Earth Charter which was proposed at Rio. During the world conference itself, the Council organized a major ecumenical gathering under the theme "Searching for the New Heavens and the New Earth". It was held in Baixada Fluminense, a community outside Rio where the ways in which issues of economics, environment and race take human shape in people's daily lives is vividly evident. Since the Earth Summit, the major focus of the Coun-

cil's engagement in this area has been the international work towards a convention on climate change (*see separate article*).

The WCC's involvement in the world conference on **population** and development in Cairo in September 1994 brought to light significant differences on a number of controversial issues within the ecumenical community. These differences were thrown into sharp relief by the firm defence of official Roman Catholic teaching on birth control by the Vatican delegation (whose status in UN deliberations is not that of an accredited NGO, like the WCC, but of a non-member state, through the representation of

NG FOR THE NEW HEAVENS AND THE NEW EARTH
AN ECUMENICAL RESPONSE TO THE EARTH SUMMIT

BUSCANDO NOVO CÉU E NOVA TERRA
UMA RESPOSTA ECUMÊNICA À CÚPULA DA TERRA

BUSCANDO NUEVO CIELO Y NUEVA TIERRA
NA RESPUESTA ECUMÉNICA A LA CUMBRE DE LA TIERRA

the Holy See). A 25-person international delegation represented the WCC in Cairo; subsequently, they produced a study document for member churches on the issues raised.

At the world summit on **social development** held in Copenhagen in March 1995, the WCC's involvement included a presentation to the conference plenary session by general secretary Konrad Raiser, who drew on ecumenical social reflection and the experience of churches around the world to raise pointed questions about the enthusiasm in many quarters for "sustainable growth".

Vienna was the site in June 1995 of the world conference on **human rights**. High on the agenda there was the growing dispute about the issue of whether human rights are in fact "universal" or whether the standards set forth in documents like the Universal Declaration of Human Rights reflect Western understandings growing out of the European Enlightenment. Again for this meeting, the Council convened a series of regional meetings to help prepare positions to be represented at the conference itself.

At the world conference on **women** and development in Beijing in August 1995, the WCC sponsored attendance by several women from churches around the world and in China, and animated several workshops in the NGO forum alongside the intergovernmental conference. Presentations at one of those workshops, in which women reflected on how cultural norms and practices affect their situation, were subsequently published as part of the WCC's pamphlet series on Gospel and Cultures in preparation for the world conference on mission and evangelism.

A review of WCC involvement in these five conferences drew a number of lessons for the future. On the positive side, it was noted that the conferences were of a high political calibre, sought to link issues with those addressed at previous conferences, provided for a strong representation by NGOs, and showed greater willingness than earlier such gatherings to make commitments and move towards agreements in international law rather than merely adopt non-binding resolutions, thus providing opportunities for follow-up.

Yet many of the decisions which have the greatest impact on the peoples of the world are not taken in UN gatherings, but in other forums dominated by the wealthy countries of the North – the Group of Seven industrialized nations (G-7), the World Bank and International Monetary Fund, and the World Trade Organization. Moreover, to influence the political processes in UN conferences it is far more important to take part in the preparatory meetings than in the conferences themselves. This, however, requires a substantial commitment of time, money and energy.

The ecumenical meeting during the Earth Summit in 1992 (above) was followed five years later with a WCC-organized petition on climate change, introduced by general secretary Konrad Raiser at a press conference in Bonn, Germany.

Sharing and Service

The work of the programme unit on sharing and service has included a diversity of initiatives undertaken to express the diaconal commitment of the churches, including interchurch aid and service to uprooted people.

Jubilee people

The "service of human need" is one of the core functions of the World Council of Churches as listed in its Constitution.

Indeed, programmes of service to refugees, aid and relief made up a major part of the Council's work even before it was formally established at Amsterdam in 1948. At the outset, major attention went to providing ecumenical assistance to the vast number of people – an estimated 12 million – who had been left homeless by the second world war in Europe. But ecumenical interchurch aid soon expanded beyond Europe and beyond refugee service. As time passed, what was successively known as the Division of, then the Commission on Inter-Church Aid, Refugee and World Service came to account for what was by far the largest part of the budget of the WCC.

The idea of Christian service or *diakonia* has evolved over the years as the churches have gained new experiences and faced new situations of human need.

A useful survey of how this discussion has developed, as well as an outline of the contemporary challenges posed to the various bodies and agencies the churches have set up to deal with human need, is offered in the 1995 book *Not Angels but Agencies*, written by Michael Taylor, the former director of Christian Aid in the UK (one of the Council's partner agencies), and published in the WCC Publications Risk Book series.

In the years leading up to the Canberra assembly, the WCC had convened two major world consultations which offered new insights into ecumenical diaconal ministry – in Larnaca, Cyprus, in 1986, and in El Escorial, Spain, in 1987. Canberra reaffirmed the findings from both consultations: the call from Larnaca for an engagement in *diakonia* that reflects the need for political liberation and social transformation for those suffering from injustice, oppression and violation of their human rights; and El Escorial's "guidelines" for the ecumenical sharing of resources, which stress the need for cooperation and participation rather than competition and domination.

In the new post-Canberra structure of the WCC, diaconal concerns became the primary focus of the programme unit on Sharing and Service (Unit IV). A plan called "Strategy for Jubilee", adopted at the meeting of its commission in Alexandria, Egypt, in 1995, brought together new insights into the ecumenical understanding of diakonia and changes in the WCC's style of diaconal work which had already begun to take place.

The theme of jubilee was the topic of a good deal of reflection within the WCC throughout this period. Its source is the biblical legislation, recorded in Leviticus 25, which mandated the release of slaves, rest for the land and the return of land to its original owners during a jubilee year every 50 years. While there is no evidence that this legislation was ever put into practice in ancient Israel, the idea of "the year of the Lord's favour", with its promise of restoration, liberation and new beginnings, is found in the prophetic writings. Jesus took up these same themes in the proclamation of good news, freedom and healing in his inaugural sermon in Nazareth, recorded in Luke 4:18-21.

The vision statement for the plan, which seeks to apply the principles of the biblical jubilee to the present-day world, identifies four focal elements of the unit's task to assist member churches and related agencies "to promote human dignity and sustainable community with the marginalized and excluded". These are (1) working with the marginalized and excluded for more just sharing of resources and alternative models of cooperation; (2) practical actions of solidarity; (3) capacity-building and empowerment within communities; and (4) networking and advocacy to enable communities to speak for themselves.

Central to all this is the identification of the "jubilee people", the priority groups

A cooperative farm community in the Philippines.

whose needs and rights are to be addressed through practical actions of solidarity: children, marginalized and excluded women, people who are economically and politically marginalized, uprooted people (refugees, internally displaced people and migrants), and people in conflict and disaster situations.

Through the varied activities of its regional desks – for Africa, Asia, Europe, Latin America and the Caribbean, the Middle East and the Pacific – as well as its functional desks, which address issues (such as refugees and migration, human resource development and communication) which cut across all regions, the unit has sought to promote the cause of the jubilee people.

Structures for sharing: regional groups and round tables

The regional desks in Unit IV represent much more than just a convenient way of organizing the WCC's varied initiatives in sharing and solidarity. This division of the work reflects a growing commitment during the period since the Canberra assembly to see responsibility for and power in ecumenical diaconal action moved away from the global level and closer to those directly affected by the decisions made.

Two key structures for carrying out sharing along these lines are the Regional Groups and the Round Tables.

These two structures themselves go back to well before the Canberra assembly: the WCC established Regional Groups in 1972 and Round Tables in 1984.

The original role of the Regional Groups was to screen and list specific development projects which churches and other bodies in their region had submitted to them. A set of guidelines regarding regionalization, which the WCC and its partners agreed to in 1993, emphasized that all concerned should have a say in decisions, that processes of decision-making should be transparent and that an ecumenical discipline should be accepted by all partners – in other words a willingness to follow these procedures together in funding and implementing projects. The role of the Regional Groups increasingly came to be one of analyzing the needs of the region as a whole and making recommendations about how resources should be shared and by whom.

In order for the Regional Groups to undertake this task in as credible and inclusive a way as possible, each includes representatives from the churches and the Regional Ecumenical Organization of the region, from Northern aid and development agencies, from the WCC and from ecumenical networks and movements. They also try to involve representatives of the "jubilee people" whom they wish to assist. In addition, the group may invite movements which are not directly related to the church and specialists in particular issues to participate in its deliberations.

The function of the Regional Groups is thus to provide economic, political and social analysis of the region, to suggest guidelines and priorities for specific action, to offer advice regarding policies and projects to the churches of the region and to aid and development agencies, and to take action which can serve as model strategies for confronting regional issues.

Round Tables fulfill the same kind of function as Regional Groups, but their scope is limited to a single country. The original purpose behind them was a desire to avoid a scatter-shot approach of supporting projects which were unrelated to one another. In fact, experience over the years has shown that Round Table meetings have tended to be dominated by money matters and by the priorities of the national councils of churches which are represented on them.

During the past seven years, there were intensive reviews of both of these structures by which the WCC and its ecumenical partners seek to ensure that ecumenical resources are shared with transparency and accountability.

Particularly significant was a process called "Discerning the Way Together", in which Northern agencies related to the WCC and ecumenical partners in the South analyzed changes brought about by rapid developments in the contemporary global social, political and economic situation.

An interesting feature of this process was that it issued not one but two reports, one from the point of view of the North and one from the point of view of the South.

The report by the Northern agencies spoke of the failure of the prevailing model of development, the limited global influence of ecumenical agencies, the role of theology in the context of the agencies' work and the need for Northern and Southern partners to have common goals and mutual respect for each other's identity.

While the report from the South agreed with the North on the dimensions and nature of the world's problems, it also spoke of some advances in the contemporary situa-

Examining various sorts of potato plants at an agricultural research centre in Romania which receives technical and financial aid from the Netherlands.

tion, including recent mobilization for political emancipation, human rights and democratization, and social development reflected in the strengthening of civil society.

A review of the Round Tables in 1995 concluded that their achievements were generally questioned more often by external partners than by those in the national situation. It also found that, despite a good deal of talk about mutuality and partnership, the dependence of the churches in the South on funds from outside is continuing to hinder the realization of genuine equality among the members of the Round Tables.

Part of the problem seemed to be different expectations of the Round Tables. This could perhaps be overcome, it was suggested, by strengthening the continuing relationships between the partners, so that routine business could be conducted in this way, while the Round Table meeting itself could be devoted to airing and resolving disagreements and differences among them.

The report also observed that the goals of commitment and genuine mutuality might be enhanced if the external partners were to disclose more information about their own activities, particularly within their own countries.

Uprooted people
recovering the vocation of the church of the stranger

The decision by the WCC Central Committee to declare 1997 as an Ecumenical Year for Churches in Solidarity with Uprooted People was first and foremost an appeal to member churches to give increased attention and visibility to a concern that has been on the agenda of the World Council of Churches since the years when it was still in process of formation, more than a half-century ago. The first refugee secretary was in fact appointed to the Geneva staff in 1940; and an ecumenical committee to coordinate his efforts to resettle Jews fleeing Nazi persecution functioned from 1942 on.

At the time of the Amsterdam assembly, the chief WCC concern was how to structure a ministry of Christian service to the millions of people in Europe who had been displaced by the second world war. The World Council offered a central point to which churches seeking to aid these uprooted people could turn for legal, technical and political expertise that went beyond the capacities they had available at the national level. Not long after the Council's official founding, attention turned to the displacement of Palestinians in the conflict that erupted over the establishment of the state of Israel.

Over the years the problem has more and more become a worldwide one. Ministry to refugees has become a challenge to churches everywhere. In supporting ministries to persons who have fled their homes, as well as those who are returning home after a period of displacement, the WCC has worked closely with bodies such as the office of the United Nations High Commissioner for Refugees and with councils of churches at the regional and national levels.

Despite consistent action by churches and related groups – sometimes at considerable cost – the number of uprooted people worldwide has continued to grow, straining and often overwhelming the churches' resources. What many of those involved in earlier ecumenical assistance to refugees perhaps saw as a temporary response to an emergency situation has become a permanent and growing task.

It was this recognition – that the global situation of refugees, displaced persons and migrants is a major and urgent contemporary crisis – that lay behind the decision to identify 1997 as a year of churches in solidarity with these uprooted people.

Statistics sum up the dimensions of the current problem. Figures for 1995 provided by UN agencies suggest that around the world there were some 15 million refugees (as defined by international standards), 30 million "internally displaced persons" (those who have suddenly or unexpectedly fled their homes in the wake of armed conflict, internal strife, systematic human rights violations or disasters, but who have remained within their own countries), and 85 million international migrants. Together, they account for nearly one in every 50 human beings.

The Central Committee's decision was part of the action it took in adopting a statement entitled "A Moment to Choose: Risking to Be with Uprooted People". That document in turn reflected some 15 months of consultation and dialogue with the WCC's member churches and related agencies. At the request of the Council, more than a hundred national and international church bodies in every region contributed written submissions, based on their own experiences in ministry to uprooted people and often drawing on special consultations among their own constituents. On the basis of this input, a reference group of six church-related experts from each region drafted the text for the Central Committee.

Underlying the statement is a challenge to the churches themselves to "rediscover their identity, their integrity and their vocation as the church of the stranger". In other words, service to people who have been uprooted from their homes is not just a problem to be dealt with by specialized refugee programmes but a challenge to the very identity of every church: is it ready to be an expression of the universality of the gospel and a home to all who are seeking to claim their human dignity? "When churches close themselves to the strangers in their midst," the statement warns, "when they no longer strive for an inclusive community as a sign and foretaste of the kingdom to come, they lose their reason to be."

This challenge to the churches to be in solidarity with uprooted people is heightened by the sharp worldwide decline in "the will to provide protection for them… Governments in all regions, led by those in countries of the industrialized North, are imposing restrictive immigration controls and draconian 'deterrence measures' to prevent the arrival of asylum-seekers and migrants… A dangerous rise in racist and xenophobic hostility is often expressed in violence against refugees and immigrants.

A school basement with no running water became the new home for some of the ten thousand people fleeing the conflict between Armenia and Azerbaijan over the disputed enclave of Nagorno-Karabagh.

They frequently become scapegoats for many social and economic tensions." Meanwhile, too little attention is being given to preventing or resolving the conditions which uproot people in the first place.

The Central Committee text and an accompanying 90-page resource book prepared by the WCC's Refugee and Migration Service seek to hold together an analysis and account of the massive global dimensions of the problem with a recognition that behind the awesome statistics lie millions of individual stories of human need and suffering, courage and hope.

Defining as "uprooted" all those people who are forced to leave their homeland for political, environmental and economic reasons, the document proposes that everyone has the human right to roots: the right to remain in his or her homeland in safety and dignity. For Christians, it suggests, this affirmation is based on fundamental convictions about the sacredness of all human life and the sanctity of creation, the values of love, justice and peace, and the challenge to build inclusive community.

The Central Committee's appeal to the churches thus follows these three lines, while acknowledging that the specific actions taken will differ according to the particular context and the resources available to churches and related bodies there.

Wherever they are, WCC member churches are challenged to promote respect for uprooted people by protecting their lives and safety through shelter, sponsorship and, if necessary, sanctuary; to defend their legal and human rights; and to promote ratification and implementation of international standards. In particular, churches are urged to take part in efforts to develop international standards for the protection of internally displaced persons – who fall outside the scope of existing provisions for refugees and whose needs often go unmet precisely because they remain within their own country and external agencies are reluctant to intervene.

Working for justice and peace, according to the statement, must involve addressing the root causes of forced displacement – not only through study and analysis, but also through the churches' engagement in peacemaking and conflict resolution and building alliances with other community-based groups.

Creating community with the uprooted means providing diaconal services, support and solidarity without discrimination, the statement says. An emphasis here is on the full participation of uprooted people themselves in planning the churches' programmes and services of ministry to refugees and migrants. Specific attention should go to the situation of uprooted women and children. And churches must work with people of other faiths and other community organizations to restore public solidarity with the uprooted.

Supporting the development of human resources

The financial support which the WCC Scholarships Programme annually provides to cover tuition and living expenses for some 300 students is a tangible expression of the Council's commitment to "promote capacity-building and empowerment within communities to rediscover and develop their own potential".

In a typical year, the recipients of these scholarships come from about 90 countries, nearly all in the South. Some are theological students, but most of the awards are made for development-oriented education and for short-term courses lasting from three months to two years.

The programme aims at developing intercultural and ecumenical understanding as well as affording professional training. The recipients of WCC scholarships generally study abroad. Increasingly, they are going to countries of the South – both to strengthen educational institutions there and to decrease dependence on the North and the West.

Priority in awarding scholarships goes to women (the goal is that half the recipients each year should be women, although it has proved difficult to increase the number of applications from women candidates) and to applicants from churches where there is little local access to training opportunities. In the selection process care is taken to ensure a wide representation of denominations and church traditions.

While most of the awards in the past have gone to students from Africa, Asia, Latin America and the Pacific, the Scholarships Office has made a concerted effort during the past several years to build up a network of correspondents and national scholarships committees in the countries of Eastern Europe.

The candidates are recommended by churches and church-related organizations; and in making their application they must indicate how their proposed study is related to the service they expect to render to their church and community after completing it.

Initial screening of candidates is in the hands of national scholarship committees. The national correspondents who convene these committees serve as the link between national ecumenical bodies and the office in Geneva. Besides assisting applicants for scholarships from their own country, national correspondents provide support for WCC scholarship recipients who have come from abroad to study there.

The decision after the Canberra assembly to move the scholarships office in the WCC from the education desk to the sharing and service unit emphasized the orientation of the programme to the goal of human resource development for churches and church-related organizations. The idea is that the churches should be selecting candidates who can be expected to help them to meet their own future needs and priorities.

An external evaluation of the Scholarships Programme at the beginning of the 1990s hailed the "remarkable job" which had been done in helping churches to develop their personnel. However, it went on to observe, "there is no evidence that it has managed to encourage human resource development programmes in the churches". Ideally, scholarships would be awarded in response to specific needs for personnel development identified by churches and church-related bodies on the basis of long-term personnel planning. The actual situation among most ecumenical partners, as a report of the Scholarships Office has suggested, is that "personnel planning is scarcely done, and training is requested more or less accidentally in cases where the requesting bodies know about the Scholarships Programme".

A rapid increase in the number of scholarships awarded in the early 1990s created a short-term financial crunch for the programme, but reductions and tighter controls, as well as increased support from donors, restabilized the programme, though there are always more requests than can be met from available resources, especially for scholarships for theological study. In some cases, this situation is alleviated through free places being made available by educational institutions or by government grants for development studies.

ACT and ECLOF
emergency aid and fair credit

Through its programme unit on Sharing and Service, the WCC is closely linked with two specialized initiatives for coordinating a particular facet of the churches' involvement in diaconal service: Action by Churches Together (ACT) International and the Ecumenical Church Loan Fund (ECLOF).

The former was established in August 1995; the latter celebrated its 50th anniversary in 1996. Both address old ecumenical concerns – which have been part of the work of the Council from the outset – that have recently taken on new dimensions. As such, their status as bodies which have an identity of their own but are related closely to the WCC enables a flexible and creative response to human needs.

ACT International is a network of churches and related agencies responding to emergencies around the globe. Its coordinating office in Geneva was set up by the WCC and the Lutheran World Federation; and it is governed by a 30-member Emergency Committee, drawn from some 40 churches and related agencies around the world, which meets annually. An executive committee of six meets three times a year and is in daily contact with the coordinating office in Geneva to review emergencies and issue appeals for aid.

The decision to form ACT was an attempt to ensure greater coordination in the churches' response – with increasingly limited resources – to the growing number of emergencies worldwide. While some of these emergencies arise from immediate natural causes such as an earthquake, flood, hurricane or drought, many are complex emergencies involving war or civil conflict and bringing in their wake environmental destruction, long-term food shortages, an exodus of refugees and needs for rehabilitation.

ACT itself is not "operational". Instead, it works with implementing partners to carry out the projects of relief in response to its appeals. In 1996, for example, ACT issued 57 such appeals, raising more than US$32 million from its network for emergency response in 47 countries and territories in Africa, Asia, the Pacific, Europe, the Middle East and Latin America. The funds, raised through 32 churches and agencies, come from church offerings and private donations, as well as from governments and the European Union. Some 49 member churches and agencies were involved in delivering ACT assistance over the year.

For example, in a climate of continuing ethnic tension and conflict, ACT members in the Great Lakes Region of Africa provided refugee camp management, repatriation, reconstruction and reconciliation. In the Middle East, ACT provided food and temporary shelter for some 11,500 families in Sidon, Beirut, the Beqaa Valley and Mount Lebanon after Israeli attacks on South Lebanon, then later helped families returning to rebuild ruined homes and villages. Reconstruction was also on ACT's agenda in the former Yugoslavia, as well as providing food and medicine, psycho-social counselling and reconciliation programmes after years of war and civil conflict. More than one million US dollars' worth of rice, wheat, high protein biscuits and fortified milk were shipped through ACT to North Korea.

Sometimes ACT's involvements can be dangerous. Several ACT workers have been kidnapped in Chechnya, where food and other assistance valued at US$2.3 million were distributed in 1996.

ACT relief is distributed regardless of race, gender, creed, nationality, ethnic origin or political persuasion. ACT members are signatories to a code of conduct for disaster relief drawn up

in collaboration with the international Red Cross and Red Crescent movements. Through the WCC and LWF, ACT is part of the Steering Committee for Humanitarian Response, through which a number of nongovernmental organizations keep in regular contact to coordinate emergency responses. Especially after the Rwanda genocide in 1994, questions regarding the ethics of humanitarian relief have been given increasing attention in the ecumenical community.

As with ACT, the major work of **ECLOF** is also carried out away from Geneva, through a network of national committees, with the central office in the Ecumenical Centre serving a chiefly coordinating role.

The particular concern of ECLOF is fostering development through fair credit. The fund itself began in 1946 specifically to aid in the reconstruction of churches destroyed by the war in Europe, though its roots reach back to initiatives by several Swiss bankers in the 1920s to create a revolving fund to support church building projects internationally through loans.

Already in the 1950s, ECLOF began to investigate the possibilities of expanding its outreach beyond Europe; and national committees were set up in Burma in 1959, Tanzania in 1960 and Argentina in 1961. Loans at that time were still predominantly for building projects: schools, clinics and community centres as well as churches. After 1970, the mandate of ECLOF was

The Ethiopian Orthodox Church and its partners in Canada have provided a mill for this small village southeast of Addis Ababa.

ACT International distributed relief supplies, including food and medicine, in Somalia, after flooding in 1997 ravaged parts of the country, killing hundreds and leaving many others homeless.

extended further to allow loans to more general development projects by churches and church-related organizations. Throughout the 1980s, the emphasis came more and more to be on local empowerment and the empowerment of women.

By the mid-1990s, one focus of ECLOF's work was a reminder of where it had begun. The momentous changes in Eastern and Central Europe after the collapse of state socialism had revealed a depth of poverty and deprivation that had long been unrecognized. Churches were in desperate need of new capital funds and training; and a special fund was established for ECLOF work in the region, where people who had been liberated from political repression were now experiencing the new form of economic oppression which came with the "shock treat-

ments" and "austerity measures" involved in the "conversion" to capitalist economies.

In 1995 a statement by the WCC Central Committee affirmed the vision of ECLOF and its evolution during the first 50 years. It noted that this anniversary was taking place "at a critical moment, when it has been recognized that established economic models have failed to sustain human development, and criticism of models of aid and partnership is at its height. Persistent poverty, which impacts women and children the most, and inequitable distribution of resources make the challenge for the future even more urgent than before." The Committee called on churches and ecumenical agencies to allocate lending capital resources to support the ECLOF credit programme.

Networking and advocacy

Over the past seven years, the decision to focus the WCC's diaconal work on communities that have been marginalized and excluded has led to an increasingly explicit role for the Council in networking and advocacy. To consolidate these efforts and give them a coherent framework, a Networking and Advocacy team was created within the programme unit on Sharing and Service in 1996.

Networking and advocacy both have to do with making connections: networking so that separated communities can come to know one another and join their efforts on common concerns; advocacy so that the various local manifestations of specific problems come to the attention of those who are in a position to influence decisions and make changes.

If advocacy is to be effective, it must be carried out locally, nationally and internationally. Local advocacy involves empowering groups and communities to speak out and influence local government policies so as to improve the immediate circumstances in which people live. At the national level, advocacy means encouraging and supporting actions by national church and ecumenical organizations, as well as challenging church leaders to take part in national policy debates. Internationally, advocacy seeks to influence ecumenical, nongovernmental and intergovernmental organizations and the United Nations system.

Since building people's awareness regarding specific concerns is a central element of networking and advocacy, making appropriate use of the communication media is critical. To assist in this, the WCC's Networking and Advocacy team has continued to coordinate a global network which brings together professional communicators from ecumenical agencies and their

partners, in order to share plans and resources as well as to discuss common issues facing them.

Against the background of the violence, hatred, destruction and misery which form the substance of much of what is communicated through the mass media, a continuing emphasis is the importance of communicating signs of hope – examples and models of actions and commitments which are actually making a positive difference in people's lives.

With the rapid developments in electronic technology for communicating, the unit

Landmine removal in Angola: 1100 years of work to go.

also set up an Information Management Systems Development team to promote the sharing of information among partner networks.

Over the years, each of the WCC's regional desks has built long-term relationships with churches, ecumenical organizations and groups and other partners. That, together with the familiarity of the staff with the region, enables the WCC to play an important role as a clearing-house for information and interpretation, which gives credibility to its initiatives for advocacy in the region.

An example is the Pacific Desk. During this period it has sought to bring to ecumenical and international attention a number of the concerns of the peoples in these sparsely populated and widely scattered island nations: through an ecumenical seminar on the future of the colonized Kanak people of New Caledonia, through visits, publications and advocacy for the people of the island of Bougainville, torn by a protracted but little-known conflict over a movement to separate itself from Papua New Guinea, and, most prominently, through a range of activities designed to call international attention to the effects of nuclear weapons testing in the Pacific.

While this latter issue has long been on the ecumenical agenda, renewed attention to it was spurred by the 1995 decision of the French government to go counter to an international moratorium and undertake a series of underground tests of nuclear weapons at its site in Muroroa in French Polynesia. Rapid exchange of information was supplemented by a publicity campaign which included posters and postcards addressed to the French president. The WCC also helped to facilitate an encounter between church representatives from

French Polynesia and French President Jacques Chirac. Members of the WCC Central Committee, in session in Geneva, joined in a public march from the Ecumenical Centre to the plaza in front of the United Nations; and officers of the Committee presented the head of the UN's Geneva office with a copy of the statement it had just adopted on nuclear testing.

Subsequently, the Council helped to fund a scientific study challenging claims by the French government which minimized the environmental and health risks of its nuclear testing at the Pacific site.

In undertaking the actions in response to nuclear testing, the Pacific Desk worked closely with other partners, including a group called Europe-Pacific Solidarity.

More recently, a similarly cooperative style of work was illustrated in the Council's participation in the international campaign against landmines, whose work in moving forward an international convention to ban the production and use of these weapons was recognized by the award of the 1997 Nobel Peace Prize.

It was largely as a result of the vigorous and effective efforts by many groups, coordinated by the international campaign, that anti-personnel landmines have come to be recognized as a worldwide plague, the more dangerous because they are relatively inexpensive and they continue to maim and kill long after hostilities have ceased. At the current rate of clearing mines, it is estimated that it would take 1100 years to remove only those mines which are now in place.

Reconstruction efforts in many countries touched by recent conflicts – among them Cambodia, the former Yugoslavia and Angola – are hampered by the massive threat unexploded landmines pose to the population. Worldwide, exploding mines kill at least 800 people every month, most of them women, children and agricultural workers. The unexploded mines add to the suffering by preventing long-term resettlement of refugees and rendering good agricultural land useless, thus curtailing food supplies in areas which can least afford it. The social and economic dislocation caused by so many deaths and disabling injuries and the resulting human suffering and family grief are incalculable.

Working closely with the Lutheran World Federation, the WCC joined in making common cause with many concerned organizations and churches to pressure governments unilaterally to ban the production and use of such weapons, to declare them illegal under international law and to stigmatize them as immoral.

The WCC and children

A small consultation in Geneva in May 1996 highlighted an ecumenical concern that has been growing over the past seven years: how can churches more effectively support children in situations of vulnerability around the world?

The immediate occasion for this gathering was a mandate from the commission for the programme unit on Sharing and Service that excluded and marginalized children should be a priority concern in the WCC's networking and advocacy work. This concern had come onto the Council's agenda particularly as a result of support given by

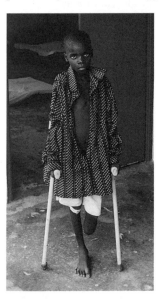

A child at one of the three institutions in Angola where rehabilitation for landmine victims is available.

the WCC's area desk for Latin America to projects for street children in that part of the world; but it is evident that, whatever their particular manifestations, the problems facing children are worldwide in scope.

Certainly the presence of street children is a worldwide phenomenon. Estimates are that 100 million children under the age of 15 live "on the streets". But other equally staggering statistics underscore the scope of the challenges facing advocacy for children. One million children are forced into prostitution every year, of whom most will contract HIV/AIDS. Of the children born with HIV infection (one million by mid-1994, and an estimated 1400 every day), 80 percent will die before they reach their fifth birthday. Chronic undernourishment is the plight of 190 million children under 5, even if only about 2 percent of them show visible signs of malnourishment. At least 200 million children work full-time, most of them on farms in South Asia. And child slaves are common in many parts of the world: in two countries alone there are said to be more than 800,000.

The Geneva consultation sought in the first place to let children speak; and the 20 adults present were joined by nine children, aged 13 to 18, from Brazil, Cameroon, Canada, Nepal, Papua New Guinea, Peru, Portugal and the USA. All of them were already working in advocacy for children in their own contexts.

The three focal points for discussion at the consultation were the areas in which those nine children have been most closely involved – child labour, child prostitution and street children. But other key issues for future church and ecumenical concern were also identified: child soldiers, war orphans and the plight of girls in war zones; refugee children; children with AIDS; female infanticide and female genital mutilation.

A report of the consultation, published under the title *We Can Help Each Other*, records some of the testimonies offered by the children present, as well as a summary of proposed responses to the issue. For the WCC, the report says, a priority should be to support the development of a global child-to-child network, whose goal would be to enforce child rights – guaranteeing the healthy physical, mental, social, cultural and spiritual development of all children. Efforts should concentrate on both meeting the short-term needs of children and on addressing the factors that contribute to the destruction of child rights. That suggests a strategy of cooperation with other groups and individuals concerned with children's issues, educating people about child rights, insisting that decision-makers place children at the top of the agenda, and finding meaningful ways to alleviate the current suffering of children.

The consultation drafted specific lists of suggestions for future work in this area by the WCC, by children, by churches and by international humanitarian organizations.

Building ties with member churches

The extensive process of study and consultation "Towards a Common Understanding and Vision of the World Council of Churches" has emphasized the fundamental identity of the WCC as a *fellowship of churches*.

While there are various ways of understanding the theological and ecclesiological implications of that definition, which is drawn from the constitutional Basis of the Council, its consequences in organizational terms are evident: the WCC is a membership body. Thus, developing, monitoring and strengthening the ties that link the Council's Geneva offices and its governing bodies with its member churches around the world is an essential ongoing concern.

The responsibility for maintaining these relationships is so all-encompassing that it obviously cannot be delegated to a single office. To do so would, indeed, contradict the insight that the essence of the WCC is to be a fellowship of churches, not an agency carrying on activities apart from its member churches.

Nevertheless, monitoring relationships with 330 churches in over 100 countries in a coordinated fashion does require specific and focused attention; and for this reason an Office of Church and Ecumenical Relations was established as part of the new WCC structure in January 1992.

The task of strengthening the quality of the fellowship in the WCC is complicated not only by the number and geographical spread of the member churches but also by the great variety of local situations in which they live and the critical moments they may be passing through.

With a small staff and a wide-ranging mandate (of which maintaining relations with member churches is only one part), the office works in constant collaboration with groups and individuals within the staff – regional and other task forces, area desks in the Sharing and Service unit, other staff whose programmatic activities bring them in contact with member churches – as well as with partners outside.

No doubt the most effective way to build relationships is through person-to-person encounters with representatives of member churches, either when they visit the Ecumenical Centre in Geneva or during official visits to their churches by the general secretary, other WCC staff or ecumenical delegations. Some encounters of this kind are pastoral visits to express solidarity with churches in situations of rapid social and political change (for example, in Eastern and Central Europe) or of conflict (such as in the former Yugoslavia). In other cases

(Syria, Angola, Malaysia have been recent examples) the motive is to strengthen or rekindle relationships with member churches.

In visits of this kind, the Office of Church and Ecumenical Relations often collaborates with other parts of the Council. That was particularly the case in the most intensive visiting programme undertaken within the Council during this period: the series of team visits planned in connection with the Ecumenical Decade of Churches in Solidarity with Women, which aimed to visit each of the Council's member churches.

A new strategy for building relations with member churches has been to draw "ecumenical officers" – persons assigned specific responsibilities for a church's ecumenical relations – into a network linked with the WCC. At a first meeting in 1996 participants drew up a working document for such a network; and the office has subsequently established regular contact with its members through letters and by sharing reports and other documents.

Relations with the WCC's Orthodox member churches have had high priority throughout these years. The Orthodox churches understand themselves as a single family whose tradition gives them a profile, an understanding of the church, and a style of worship, theology and church life which

During a visit to Switzerland in 1995, Ecumenical Patriarch Bartholomeos spoke at the Ecumenical Centre and celebrated liturgy at the Orthodox centre nearby in Chambésy.

Relationships

The Council's two relationships offices, a new element in the post-Canberra structure, have worked to coordinate both the WCC's relations with churches and other ecumenical bodies and its relations with people and organizations of other faiths.

distinguish them from the Protestant churches which were dominant in the formation of the WCC and have remained so throughout its history.

These differences, along with differences of language and the political restrictions under which many Orthodox churches have lived throughout their history and especially during most of the 20th century, have always coloured the Orthodox presence within the fellowship of the WCC. Developments after the end of Communist rule in Eastern and Central Europe have tended to heighten tensions and misunderstandings.

A declaration by the Orthodox participants in the Canberra assembly raised a number of critical theological and organizational questions about the WCC and the implications of these for their membership in the Council. When Metropolitan Bartholomeos (later elected Ecumenical Patriarch) read this statement at the assembly, he underscored that it was made out of a concern for and loyalty to the fellowship in the Council; but many observers tended to put more emphasis on the declaration as a thinly veiled warning of imminent Orthodox withdrawal from the WCC.

The issues taken up in that statement formed the basis of an inter-Orthodox consultation in Chambésy later in 1991; and several other such encounters, formal and informal, followed during this period.

The Office of Church and Ecumenical Relations devoted considerable time to advising colleagues in the WCC about activities and programmes related to Orthodox churches, including team visits to Orthodox churches in the context of the Ecumenical Decade. It has also assisted in preparing visits by the general secretary to nearly all Orthodox member churches, as well as organizing visits by primates of a number of Orthodox churches to the Ecumenical Centre.

The office also focused on a number of specific issues which have come to trouble Orthodox churches in the post-Communist period: the situation regarding the Eastern Catholic or uniate churches and the tensions arising from what is seen as proselytism by mission agencies from outside. In connec-

What WCC membership means

Elements of what it means for a church to belong to the WCC are summarized in the Central Committee's 1997 policy document "Towards a Common Understanding and Vision of the World Council of Churches". According to that statement, to be a member of the WCC means:

– nurturing the ability to pray, live, act and grow together in community with churches from differing backgrounds and traditions, dealing with disagreement through theological discussion, prayer and dialogue, treating contentious issues as matters for common theological discernment rather than political victory;

– helping one another to be faithful to the gospel, and questioning one another if any member is perceived to move away from the fundamentals of the faith or obedience to the gospel;

– participating in ministries that extend beyond the boundaries and possibilities of any single church and being ready to link one's own specific local context with the global reality and to allow that global reality to have an impact in one's local situation;

– being part of a fellowship that has a voice of its own: while churches are free to choose whether or not to identify themselves with the voice of the WCC when it speaks, they are committed to giving serious consideration to what the Council says or does on behalf of the fellowship as a whole;

– making a commitment to implement in one's own church the agreements reached through joint theological study and reflection by the total fellowship;

– participating in a fellowship of sharing and solidarity, supporting other members in their needs and struggles, celebrating with them their joys and hopes;

– understanding the mission of the church as a joint responsibility shared with others, rather than engaging in missionary or evangelistic activities in isolation from each other, much less in competition with or proselytism of other Christian believers;

– entering into a fellowship of worship and prayer with the other churches, nurturing concrete opportunities for shared worship and prayer while respecting the limitations imposed by specific traditions;

– taking a full part in the life and work of the WCC and its activities, including praying for the Council and all its member churches, being represented at assemblies, making regular financial contributions to its work according to one's possibilities and sharing the WCC's concerns with local parishes, congregations and worshipping communities.

Patriarch Alexei II of the Russian Orthodox Church is welcomed to the WCC offices by general secretary Konrad Raiser for his first official visit to the Council in 1995.

tion with the former, the WCC helped to organize several team visits to areas of conflict, leading eventually to a Central Committee statement addressing ecumenical and pastoral dimensions of this problem.

A major emphasis of the work with Orthodox churches has been exposing young Orthodox theologians and lay persons to the ecumenical movement. Seminars were organized for young lecturers and exchange visits for groups of seminary stu-dents, both in predominantly Orthodox countries and in Protestant environments. This effort takes on special importance in view of the strong and growing anti-ecu-menical sentiments especially in Orthodox churches in Eastern and Central Europe.

The Office of Church and Ecumenical Relations is also responsible for preparing applications for WCC membership for pre-sentation to the governing bodies. In that connection, it held extensive consultations during this period as part of a review of the criteria for WCC membership and the meaning of membership. As a result of the former, the Central Committee adopted sev-eral changes to the rules of the WCC; in connection with the latter, it approved for study by the churches a document setting out "the meaning of membership", which was subsequently incorporated into the final policy document on Common Understand-ing and Vision (*see accompanying story*).

Reaching out to churches that are not WCC members

The WCC Central Committee sent a dis-cussion document to the churches in 1996 which elaborates what membership of the World Council means.

No comparable text sets forth the mean-ing of *non*-membership. Yet even if church membership statistics are imprecise and dif-ficult to compare, no one would seriously question that the great majority of Chris-tians in the world belong to churches which are *not* WCC members.

Most of them are Roman Catholics. But researchers suggest that even among Chris-tians who are not Roman Catholics the number belonging to WCC member churches is, or will soon be, the minority.

The rapid growth in evangelical, Pente-costal and independent churches, the latter especially in Africa, has led the WCC increasingly to recognize the importance of building relationships beyond its member churches if it is to remain true to its voca-tion as a worldwide servant of the one ecu-menical movement.

The significance of relations with these churches was singled out in the resolution by which the Central Committee mandated the Common Understanding and Vision (CUV) process in 1989; and the CUV pol-icy document approved by the Central Committee in 1997 devotes a section to relations with the Roman Catholic Church and with evangelical, Pentecostal and inde-pendent churches.

It is clear that this is not seen as a mem-bership recruitment campaign. The issue of possible Roman Catholic membership in the WCC was taken up in the early 1970s by the Joint Working Group (JWG) between the WCC and the Roman Catholic Church and became the subject of intensive discus-sion. In the end, the Vatican decided against applying for membership; and the issue has not seriously been on the agenda since then. Neither side considers it a priority at pre-

Konrad Raiser meets with Pope John Paul II and Cardinal Edward Cassidy, president of the Pontifical Council for Promoting Christian Unity, at the Vatican in 1995.

sent; and the new *Ecumenical Directory* released by the Pontifical Council for Pro-moting Christian Unity in 1995 specifically disavows any link between increasing Catholic membership in national councils of churches and Catholic membership in the WCC.

For evangelical and Pentecostal churches the obstacles to WCC membership are dif-ferent. Sometimes persistent tensions – or stereotypes – rooted in the historic "evan-gelical-ecumenical" split continue to make exploration of WCC membership counter-productive. In other cases, the churches involved do not have the kind or degree of organization that readily fits into the WCC's structure.

For the Office of Church and Ecumenical Relations, the Joint Working Group is the major focus of relations with the Roman Catholic Church. Its annual meetings review the full range of collaboration between Geneva and Rome, the ecumenical situation in every part of the world and the plans and priorities of each of the partners. During the past period, the group has devoted sustained attention to the Common Understanding and Vision process.

Besides, the JWG regularly undertakes studies of current ecumenical issues. Since the Canberra assembly reports of three such studies have been released – on ecumenical formation, on ethical issues as a source of division among the churches, and on com-mon witness and proselytism.

The very mandate of the JWG to oversee collaboration between the two partners makes clear that it is in concrete activities that WCC-Roman Catholic relations take shape. The most developed case of such collaboration is in the area of Faith and Order. The Vatican names 12 Catholic the-ologians to the 120-member Faith and Order Commission, and works together with the WCC to prepare annual materials for the Week of Prayer for Christian Unity.

A rally of the Universal Church of God's Kingdom, one of the rapidly growing Pentecostal churches in Latin America, in Rio de Janeiro, Brazil.

But there are numerous other cases of continuing cooperation, including the presence of Roman Catholic staff in the mission and evangelism section and the Ecumenical Institute at Bossey and regular contacts in such areas as interfaith relations, refugees and migration, and health.

While maintaining contacts with international evangelical organizations like the World Evangelical Fellowship and World Vision International, the Office of Church and Ecumenical Relations has also sought to build up more direct relations with churches from the evangelical and Pentecostal families, normally seeking to do this

on a regional level in cooperation with ecumenical bodies there.

A first consultation of this type was organized with evangelical free churches in Latin America. Held in November 1993 in Quito, Ecuador, the consultation was an experimental exercise in mutual listening and learning which proved to be a successful model for several subsequent encounters.

A separate consultation was held with Latin American Pentecostals in Lima, Peru, a year later. Further consultations took place with evangelical and Pentecostal African and African-Caribbean churches in the

United Kingdom (Leeds, November 1995) and with North American Pentecostals, to which some Latin American Pentecostals were also invited (San José, Costa Rica, June 1996). An international meeting in Geneva in November 1997 took stock of the developing relations in this area and proposed formation of a joint working group between the WCC and Pentecostal churches after the Harare assembly.

During the Canberra assembly, a few Orthodox and evangelical members of the newly elected Central Committee began to explore the possibility of dialogue between these two families within the WCC constituency. In January 1994 this group asked the Office of Church and Ecumenical Relations to help organize a wider Orthodox-Evangelical consultation, which took place in Alexandria, Egypt, in July 1995. The meeting was marked by a sincere openness and desire to learn from each other and to discuss differences in a spirit of Christian dialogue; and a second such encounter was planned for mid-1998.

A number of applications for WCC membership from African Instituted Churches led to the idea of opening up a more general dialogue with these churches. An initial consultation in Ogere, Nigeria, in January 1996, brought together representatives of these churches with leaders of some "historic" or "mission-founded" churches in West Africa. The office has also established a regular relationship with the Organization of African Instituted Churches in Nairobi.

Councils of churches and world communions

A key emphasis of the Common Understanding and Vision process is that the one ecumenical movement, with its many organizational manifestations, is not a kind of pyramid, but rather a many-centred network linking together bodies of different (and sometimes overlapping) constituencies and mandates. Although the WCC is not to be understood as the centre of this network, its worldwide extent and its openness to all Christian traditions give it a special opportunity to work for coordination and coherence among the many ecumenical partners.

This partnership with other ecumenical organizations, which the WCC has always acknowledged, has taken on more importance as the number of such bodies has grown. And nearly all member churches of the WCC are also affiliated with one or

more other organizations working for church unity.

For the Office of Church and Ecumenical Relations this partnership focuses on four types of bodies: national councils of churches (NCCs; sometimes called national Christian councils), regional ecumenical organizations (REOs), Christian World Communions (CWCs) and specialized international ecumenical organizations.

The WCC helped to organize the third international consultation of NCCs, held in Hong Kong in 1993 (earlier ones took place in 1971 and 1986). This was followed up by a plenary session on local and national ecumenism at the 1994 Central Committee meeting and by the development of a set of guidelines for WCC-NCC relations, approved by the

Central Committee at its meeting in 1995.

One factor that gives NCCs particular ecumenical significance is that national Roman Catholic bishops conferences have sought membership in a growing number of them (about half of the nearly 100 NCCs around the world). The Roman Catholic Church (which is also a member of the regional ecumenical bodies for the Pacific, Middle East and Caribbean) is not a member of the WCC.

A message to the Hong Kong consultation from Cardinal Edward Cassidy, head of the Pontifical Council for Promoting Christian Unity, called attention to some of the difficulties posed if the other churches in a council fail to see that their Catholic partners can work with them only "within the framework of the communion of faith and discipline of the whole Catholic Church". In particular, problems may arise when NCCs act or speak out on difficult ethical and moral questions without "due regard for the moral teaching of the member churches".

During this period national ecumenical bodies in Britain, Canada and Australia underwent significant changes in the process of incorporating Catholic membership. The shift was described by one speaker in Hong Kong in terms of the NCC's no longer existing "to do things on behalf of the churches" but rather being "the place where churches do things together as an exercise in and foretaste of the unity to come". But other observers fear that this model for ecumenism at the national level could seriously limit the relevance and pioneering role of the NCC. Even in the age of rapid communication, they ask, is it not inevitable that consulting with all member churches before saying anything publicly will always delay, often water down and sometimes eliminate a common witness on burning issues of the day?

In addition to collaboration in many of the WCC's activities, relations with regional ecumenical organizations and

Christian World Communions have been conducted through annual meetings of the general secretaries of such organizations, as well as a round of meetings between senior WCC staff and staff of each of the regional bodies. The WCC's Common Understanding and Vision process was a significant part of the agenda for many of these discussions.

The Council's collaboration with the organizations of Christian World Communions varies considerably, in part because of the differences among these bodies themselves. Historically, the greatest degree of contact has been with the two CWCs whose central offices are in the Ecumenical Centre in Geneva: the Lutheran World Federation and the World Alliance of Reformed Churches.

An important item on the agenda of the annual meetings of the general secretaries of CWCs – in which the WCC and the Pontifical Council for Promoting Christian Unity take part – has been plans for activities around the arrival of the year 2000. Already in 1994 the WCC Executive Committee urged that churches celebrating this year should do so ecumenically, that the pri-

mary focus for such ceremonies should be local and national and that the role of the WCC should be to encourage these rather than to undertake a global celebration.

Especially after the publication of Pope John Paul's encyclical on the new millennium, *Tertio millennio adveniente*, and the establishment by the Catholic Church of various preparatory commissions and materials, the meeting of CWC general secretaries became a useful forum for discussing how worldwide celebrations of the year 2000 could bring out the ecumenical dimension encouraged by both the WCC and the papal message.

An idea which emerged out of the Common Understanding and Vision process has been discussed with various ecumenical partners: that of creating a forum bringing together representatives of all ecumenical organizations for consultation and collaboration. In part, this was a response to a growing sense that the succession of large international ecumenical assemblies was proving unmanageable for churches affiliated with more than one of these bodies and thus poor stewardship of shrinking resources.

Inter-religious relations

The WCC's Office on Inter-Religious Relations succeeded the subunit on Dialogue with People of Living Faiths when the Council's new programme structure came into effect in January 1992. Focusing less on ongoing organization of interfaith dialogues, the office encourages and enables churches in their own relations with neighbours of other faiths, monitors developments in inter-religious relations, and responds to specific interfaith issues and situations of conflict in which religion plays a role.

During these years the awareness of religious plurality has grown in most parts of the world. There have been some notable initiatives to celebrate the enrichment this brings to human communities, most visibly at the international level in the 1993 centenary of the World Parliament of Religions in Chicago, which issued a much-publicized call for a "global ethic". Yet there seems to have been even more evidence of how unhealed rifts between people of different faiths can fuel conflicts and violence. Though some would dispute the use of the term "religious fundamentalism", few would disagree that renewed seriousness about religious convictions worldwide has

provided surprising and often troublesome challenges in what many had considered a secular age.

To respond to these new challenges the WCC has maintained its engagement with communities of other faiths, primarily Jews, Muslims and (though restricted during this period by staff limitations) adherents of Asian religions.

Responding to a policy paper adopted by

A 1994 meeting of Christian leaders from the former USSR with representatives of other faiths: Akhmed Salikhovitch Tagaev, deputy mufti of Dagestan, and Russian Orthodox Metropolitan Kirill of Smolensk and Kaliningrad.

the Central Committee in 1992, the Council's initiatives in Jewish-Christian dialogue took some new directions, moving beyond the European and North American context. In addition to an African Christian-Jewish consultation on the themes of "family, community and tradition", two significant Christian-Jewish encounters were co-sponsored with ecumenical partners in Asia. One, in Hong Kong, focused on the role of wisdom in the Jewish, Christian and Chinese traditions; the other, in South India, explored facets of the idea of being the "people of God" in the light of Jewish experience and Asian Christian experience – how to live as a minority, how to understand one's own faith in a world of religious plurality, what it means that humanity is created in the image of God.

A major area in which people of religion are challenged to work together for peace is the Middle East. The city of Jerusalem, sacred to Jews, Christians and Muslims, has become a symbol of both the hopes and the obstacles. With this in mind, the WCC joined the Pontifical Council for Interreligious Dialogue, the Holy See's Commission for Religious Relations with the Jews and the Lutheran World Federation in sponsoring two colloquiums on Jerusalem. (Interestingly, financial support for one of these came from the Japanese lay Buddhist movement Rissho Kosei Kai.)

The first colloquium, "The Spiritual Significance of Jerusalem for Jews, Christians and Muslims", was held in May 1993 in Glion, Switzerland. It brought together Jews, Christians and Muslims mainly from Israel, the West Bank and Gaza. Significantly, this meeting took place before the Oslo agreement rekindled hopes for a peaceful settlement of the strife between Israel and its Arab neighbours.

But by the time of the next colloquium – in Thessaloniki, Greece, in August 1996 – the vision of peace was faltering and there was pessimism in the air. Attempts to envision the future of Jerusalem did not materialize. The message spoke of Jerusalem as "a place of encounter between God and humanity and among human beings in their diversity". But although Jerusalem is "called to be the City of Peace, at the moment there is no peace... There is still a long way to go before a just and lasting peace is achieved."

Christians in a number of countries with Muslim majorities have expressed concern about what the introduction and application of Islamic law or *shari'ah* imply for the status of the Christian community in such situations. Recognizing this, the WCC organized a number of encounters with Muslims around the issue of religion and law.

The first of these meetings was, in many ways, a ground-breaking initiative. Unlike many dialogues which aim at a comparative approach to religion and society and bring together like-minded partners from both sides, the Muslim partners in this consultation in Geneva in December 1992 were people seriously committed to the application

of *shari'ah*. The discussions, while amicable, were open and candid; and divergences were not covered up.

One item discussed was the mutual misunderstanding between Muslims and Christians when they talk about the state. Christians tend to see the application of *shari'ah* as turning the state into a retrogressive theocracy, while many Muslims committed to *shari'ah* know very little about classical or modern Christian thinking on the state. The "secular" state has long been idealized by Christians in many parts of the world. But how have secular states in fact handled the question of religious minorities? Does their tendency to treat religion as an individual and private matter make them an appropriate model for the future?

Relations with Hindu and Buddhist dialogue partners were somewhat restricted not only because of staff limitations during this period, as noted above, but also by the absence of global organizations for these Asian religions and by the diversity within each.

The question of who should be the partners for Hindu-Christian dialogue has become a complicated one in the light of recent developments in Hinduism and a growing sense of Hindu self-assertion – expressed in the conflict surrounding a mosque in Ayodhya, India, and its eventual destruction by Hindu militants in December 1992. Further tensions surround the ongo-

ing mistreatment of the Dalits, those millions of Indians born outside the caste system and thus marginalized by society despite legal and constitutional measures to remove this discrimination. Christians engaged in dialogue with Hinduism are sometimes criticized for dealing with what is perceived to be the oppressive side of Hinduism. Moreover, relations with Hinduism are coloured by a preoccupation, mainly in the West, with certain aspects of Hinduism linked to the guru movement, neo-Hindu sects and various "New Age" expressions.

The WCC joined the National Council of Churches in India in arranging two workshops on Hindu-Christian relations in 1995 (Madurai) and 1997 (Varanasi). The intent was to draw up some preliminary guidelines for Hindu-Christian relations. It was suggested that Christians need to address the question of the uniqueness of Christ, the saving value of other religions, the role of the church and the relationship between dialogue and proclamation. On the part of Hindus there is a need to address the suspicion that Christians have a hidden agenda and that the ultimate loyalty of Indian Christians is not to India but to the West.

An inter-religious team-visit to Fiji in 1994 assisted a local interfaith group in addressing problems between Christian Fijians and Indians in Fiji, who are mostly Hindu or Muslim.

Two Buddhist monks at the magnificent Shwemawdaw pagoda in Bago, east of Yangon, Myanmar.

Communicating the WCC and the ecumenical movement

The mandate the Central Committee gave to the Office of Communication in 1991 starts with an overarching task: "to interpret and promote the life and work of the WCC and the ecumenical movement to the public at large and to the WCC member churches in particular".

In many cases, "interpreting" the WCC also requires preparing and disseminating *information* about the many diverse activities of the Council. Promoting "the *life and work* of the WCC *and the ecumenical movement*" extends the subject matter well beyond what is being done by the Council's central offices in Geneva – to the churches that make up this worldwide fellowship and to the numerous organizations and initiatives to foster and express Christian unity which are the WCC's indispensable partners. And the rapid global expansion of media communication means that, in both "the public at large" and WCC member churches, the message the Council communicates must compete for attention with many other messages.

The task of communicating the WCC is a continuous one. Indeed, former general secretary Philip Potter once described the WCC itself as an "organ of communication". In that sense, communicating the Council is a job the Office of Communication shares with all parts of the staff and with those responsible for communication in member churches and ecumenical bodies.

Its own specific focus is on communicating the WCC through public media – print, audiovisual and electronic – and its work is of two types: producing materials and building relations with communication media outside the Council. In doing so since the Canberra assembly, the Office of Communication has faced the same financial constraints as the Council as a whole.

The consequences of this were evident in the discontinuation of the monthly magazine *One World*. Launched in November 1974 to "draw Christians from many different continents and traditions together", the magazine sought for 21 years to interpret the WCC and to provide a platform for the diversity of experiences and convictions within the churches worldwide. *One World* published its last issue in December 1995, after a decision that the resources being devoted to a single printed product in only one language, whose circulation was declining, should instead be allocated to a more flexible, open and innovative strategy for meeting the needs of both the Council and its constituents. But planning for such new endeavours had to be put on hold when

Interpreting ecumenical concerns to media representatives: a press conference on Aboriginal and indigenous issues at the WCC's seventh assembly in Canberra, 1991.

serious shortfalls in WCC income obliged additional budget-cutting.

One World, whose disappearance many lamented, illustrated some key dilemmas of ecumenical communication. Its small staff and budget ruled out a sustained investment in promoting subscriptions. Its audience was too widely scattered and not large enough to attract the substantial advertising revenues on which many mass-circulation magazines depend. Even though its income was not expected to cover more than the costs of production and mailing, its subscription price was still too high for persons in many parts of the world. Its attempt to do justice to the full spectrum of ecumenical concerns limited its attractiveness for many who were primarily committed to one particular part of that agenda. Most of all, the fact that it appeared only in English restricted the chances of its ever achieving a foothold outside certain countries and regions.

A WCC publication even more venerable than *One World* also disappeared during this period. But when *Ecumenical Press Service*, whose roots lay in the International Christian Press and Information Service begun in the 1930s, ceased publication in September 1994, it was imme-

diately succeeded by the appearance of *Ecumenical News International* (*ENI*).

Since then *ENI* – which the WCC launched with three other international church bodies whose offices are in the Ecumenical Centre in Geneva (the Conference of European Churches, Lutheran World Federation and World Alliance of Reformed Churches) – has established itself as a leading source of international religious news. Daily dispatches, distributed to media clients in English or French by telefax or electronic mail, are collected in a biweekly printed bulletin in both languages. Used by media clients whose deadlines do not require the daily service, the bulletin is also read by many church leaders. An English summary of each day's news is also made available without charge by electronic mail.

To supplement its small Geneva staff, *ENI* has correspondents around the world and exchange arrangements with a number of outlets in Latin America. Through its media clients it is also locally translated and reproduced in parts of Asia and Africa.

ENI grew out of a recognition by the four founding partners that the work and mission of the church and the ecumenical movement are not well-known in either secular or church-related media today. Achieving this would require two things: timely distribution of professionally written news stories about events, issues and trends; and a clear distinction of this activity from the efforts of each institution to present itself to the media. Besides giving *ENI* an identity of its own, distinct from that of the four partners, this collaboration has enabled them to reduce duplication and overlap of services.

Rapid technological developments, especially in the use of computers and computer networks by the WCC and its ecumenical partners, have brought innovations in the work of all sections of the Office of Communication during the past seven years. At the same time, awareness has grown that ways must be found to extend this potential so that it does not simply reinforce the advantages of those who are already privileged and powerful.

During this period the WCC was communicated through outside media by way of numerous press releases and press conferences, as well as media operations at such major events as the six Central Committee meetings and the two world conferences on Faith and Order and on Mission and Evangelism. The Visual Arts section continued to build up a library of ecumenical photographs and video footage, and was involved in the production of several videos. WCC Publications released about 20 new books and four issues of the journal *The Ecumenical Review* each year.

In January 1998 work began in earnest on upgrading the WCC's hitherto rudimentary presence on the WorldWideWeb and exploring the multitude of possibilities for using the Internet as a vehicle for communicating the Council and its concerns. Efforts are being made in developing the WCC Web site to provide a genuinely multilingual vehicle of communication.

However, the issue of language has been a growing and unresolved preoccupation throughout the 1990s. If the WCC is primarily a fellowship of churches, as the Common Understanding and Vision document asserts, the languages of the WCC are the hundreds of languages used in its member churches. For practical reasons, the Council as an organization uses five working languages: English, French, German, Russian and Spanish. While all are European, the legacy of European colonialism means that these are the languages most likely to be spoken as second languages in WCC member churches around the world.

Translation and interpretation for Russian have historically been carried out via arrangements with the Russian Orthodox Church; the other four are the responsibility of the Language Service within the Office of Communication. Its work consists of translating WCC texts and documents, revising translation work done by outside translators and organizing interpretation for about 30 meetings and consultations every year.

The Language Service – and thus the Council's effective operation as a multilingual organization – have been hard hit by the financial difficulties of the past seven years, leading to severe staff reductions. This diminished availability of staff resources and the high costs of securing adequate translation and interpretation inevitably create pressures to reduce the number of languages used in WCC activities – often, not surprisingly, to English only. What cannot be neglected are the serious repercussions such "pragmatic" decisions have on adhering to WCC policies and honouring ecumenical principles about inclusiveness and participation.

The WCC library

As a resource for students, scholars and staff and as an "ecumenical memory bank", the World Council of Churches' library plays a quiet but important role in the ecumenical movement.

This role has been enhanced by continuous acquisition of ecumenical books and periodicals produced throughout the world in many languages, an upgrading of its computer system and strengthened links with other research libraries with the aim of extending access to its facilities.

Besides helping users to gain access to its own collection of more than 105,000 books and pamphlets on ecumenical topics, the library staff offer a range of services from compiling indexes and bibliographies to providing consultative services to other theological libraries. Related to the main WCC library at the Ecumenical Centre is a smaller facility located at the Ecumenical Institute in Bossey, whose collection is primarily intended for the use of the annual Graduate School of Ecumenical Studies.

Like other sections of the WCC, the library has in recent years been confronted with serious staff reductions due to financial limitations. Although it is the custodian of a vast quantity of archival materials documenting the history of the WCC and other ecumenical bodies, the library has been unable to fill the post of archivist for more than a year; and the director of the library has taken over responsibilities for preservation and classification of the archives and access to them.

In 1997 a specialist firm in Leiden, the Netherlands, published nearly 1500 microfiches representing the general correspondence of the WCC general secretariat archives housed by the library.

New member churches 1991-1998

Anglican Province of the Southern Cone (1995)
Autocephalous Orthodox Church of Albania (1994)
*Christian Biblical Church [Argentina] (1997)
Christian Church of East Timor (1995)
Church of the Province of Burundi (1994)
Church of the Province of Rwanda (1994)
Evangelical Lutheran Church in the Republic of Namibia (1992)
*Evangelical Pentecostal Mission of Angola (1995)
Evangelical Reformed Church of Angola (1995)
Jamaica Baptist Union (1995)
*Kenya Evangelical Lutheran Church (1995)
Methodist Church in Togo (1996)
Native Baptist Church of Cameroon (1995)
Presbyterian Community of Kinshasa, Zaire (1996)
Protestant Church in Sabah (1995)
Protestant Church in West Indonesia (1991)
Protestant Church in South-East Sulawesi (1991)
Reformed Church in Zambia (1991)
United Church of Christ-Congregational in the Marshall Islands (1992)
United Church in the Solomon Islands (1997)
United Church in Papua New Guinea (1997)
Uniting Reformed Church in Southern Africa (1995)

* Indicates associate member churches (membership of fewer than 25,000).

Ecumenical Institute, Bossey

A colloquium in honour of Nikos Nissiotis was one of the special events organized in 1996 to celebrate the 50th anniversary of the Ecumenical Institute in Bossey. The late Orthodox theologian and active ecumenist – who also coached the Greek national basketball team and was a key figure in the Olympic movement – was one of those who left their mark during the first 50 years of the Institute, which he directed during the 1970s.

Established even before the official founding of the World Council of Churches, Bossey was described by the WCC's first general secretary W.A. Visser 't Hooft as a "laboratory" for the whole ecumenical movement – a place set apart where ideas can be tested, different elements brought together and new things can emerge. The same image was used by Hans-Ruedi Weber as the title for his history of the Institute released in 1996.

How Bossey might adapt and renew itself on the eve of the 21st century – when the need for ecumenical learning is evident but the resources for it, both human and financial, are scarce – was a central theme of the Nissiotis consultation.

Since 1952 the centrepiece of the Institute's programme has been the annual four-month graduate school of ecumenical studies, in which 50-60 students from around the world are brought together for an intensive residential educational experience. Classroom lectures and traditional academic work such as writing papers blend with more experiential forms of learning which include sharing and worship across cultural and confessional divisions.

Each session of the graduate school focuses on an ecumenically topical subject. During the period between Canberra and Harare these have included inclusive community and overcoming violence, as well as the themes of the WCC's world conferences on Faith and Order (koinonia in faith, life

A cross-section of the international student body at the 1994-95 Graduate School of the Ecumenical Institute, Bossey.

and witness) and Mission and Evangelism (gospel and cultures).

Throughout the rest of the year, while the graduate school is not in session, Bossey organizes shorter courses and consultations on subjects that arise in the work of the WCC and the ecumenical movement. A regular annual feature is the weeklong course around the time of the Orthodox Easter celebration which offers an introduction to Orthodox theology and spirituality for members of other Christian churches. In 1992, for the first time, this Bossey course was in fact held in an Orthodox setting – in Romania.

Roman Catholic participation in the programmes of Bossey has increased over the years; and since 1989 the Pontifical Council for Promoting Christian Unity has seconded a Catholic educator to the Bossey teaching staff. Each graduate school programme includes a visit to the Vatican.

Many of the shorter Bossey seminars during recent years have dealt with issues related to the participation of women in the church. One of these, to which leading feminist theologians from different contexts and traditions around the world were invited, led to the publication of a collection of essays by the WCC under the title *Women's Visions: Theological Reflection, Celebration, Action.*

A Christian-Jewish dialogue meeting at Bossey resulted in a publication of essays on the theme of jubilee.

Bossey is the venue for many WCC-related meetings. Its setting in the foothills of the Jura mountains, with a view of the snow-capped peaks of the French Alps across Lake Geneva, and narrow paths crisscrossing the surrounding fields and woods, also make it a favoured location for outside groups, who can rent the facilities for short conferences or retreats.

An overview of WCC finances, 1991-1998

"To report on the finances of the World Council of Churches during this period is to paint a picture of continuous, cumulative, growing difficulties and problems. That is, of course, merely a reflection of what many of the member churches themselves have undergone…"

If this sounds like a gloomy way to introduce a short account of WCC finances between 1991 and 1998, it is instructive to

note that these sentences in fact come from the finance report to the WCC's fifth assembly in 1975 – and would have been largely applicable at the sixth and seventh assemblies as well. And if one were to replace the words "World Council of Churches", the same sentences might be used by many other international and ecumenical organizations.

One may discuss how far this is a consequence of the nature and functioning of such

organizations, or an indication of long-term trends in church life, or a reflection of global economic circumstances. In any case, the past seven years have shown that the WCC has no choice but to adjust its life and work to changes in the world, in the churches and in the nature of its funding base.

Several chronic factors create financial difficulties for the Council. One is the narrow designation of much of its income. This means that the undesignated income (principally from the churches' membership contributions) available for the Council's basic work and for responding to new needs is inadequate.

Fluctuations in currency exchange rates have also been a constant problem. The Swiss franc, in which most of the WCC's operating expenses must be paid, has consistently strengthened against the currencies in which most income is received. Declines in WCC income are thus exaggerated. Inflation – though low in recent years – is another recurring anxiety. There has also always been an imbalance in the support coming to the Council from different geographical areas and traditions. In 1996 almost half of the WCC's member churches did not pay any membership contribution at all.

In September 1990, just before the Canberra assembly and after a period of relative financial stability going back to 1983, the Council found that it faced severe projected deficits in its operating budgets for 1991 (SFr. 6 million) and 1992 (SFr. 9 million). The worsening global economic climate and a sharp drop in the value of the US dollar against the Swiss franc required urgent action to reduce expenses – for which cutting staff (*see attached story*) was the major strategy.

Acknowledging the financial difficulties, the Canberra assembly called for increased financial support from all mem-

---

Income for the WCC falls into four basic categories:
- *undesignated income*, principally from the membership contributions of the churches;
- *general income*, provided by churches and agencies to meet the general costs of the Council's work within certain broadly defined areas;
- *designated income*, intended for specific programmes, activities or projects;
- *miscellaneous income*, from sales, rent, investments and foreign exchange gains.

WCC expenditures fall mainly under three headings:
- *staff costs*, including salaries, social benefits and pension funds;
- *operating costs*, which include all the Council's other expenses in running the organization, its activities and programmes;
- *grants*, which are funds paid out to others in connection with programmes, activities and projects.

Since the WCC is not a commercial organization, it does not have an annual "profit and loss account". Instead, the annual financial report indicates the "movements on funds" during the year, that is, the difference between the balances at the beginning of the year and at the end of the year. These are reported in three different areas: *general funds* (undesignated and general income less operating expenses), *activities funds* (income and expenditure related to specific programmes and projects, which should balance over a period of time, though not necessarily within a single year), and *other funds* (reserves, property funds and assembly funds). For a given year, the statement of movement on general funds gives a clear indication of whether the Council has made an operating surplus or deficit.

---

ber churches, especially those making no financial contribution, and the development of new sources of funds, a more dynamic investment policy, a review of budgetary policy, reduction of expenditures to the level of recurring income and the development of a regular planning process in which programme priorities, staffing levels and financial projections were integrated.

To encourage churches to make an annual membership contribution, the Central Committee adopted changes to the WCC Rules making such a contribution an obligation of membership. A minimum annual contribution (presently SFr. 1000) was set; and a "giving index" was devised, suggesting the amount each church should give relative to its size and local economic factors. To raise additional funds in the United States, the WCC set up the Ecumenical Development Initiative as a joint venture with the US National Council of Churches. Attempts were also made to increase support from newer member churches in Hong Kong, South Korea, Japan and Taiwan.

The shrinking of the WCC's financial resources during the 1990s has been mirrored in a reduction of its human resources as measured in the number of staff.

From a peak of 343 employees just before the Canberra assembly, the total had declined to 300 when the new Central Committee first met in September 1991 and to 276 by its next meeting in August 1992. After remaining stable for a year, the number began to rise again in 1994, reaching 301 by September 1995.

To cope with a further drop in the Council's income, the number of staff declined steadily thereafter, stabilizing at 237 in September 1997. About 25 percent of these persons work part-time; and the number of full-time equivalents was thus 217.

The corresponding figures for programme staff in grades 7-10 (appointed by the Central Committee) also show a reduction, though not as steep: 73 in September 1991, 68 in August 1992, 63 in September 1993, 73 in September 1995 and 61 in September 1997.

A thorough review of the WCC's overall staffing picture by the Executive Committee at its meeting in March 1992 led to the adoption of a new document on staffing procedures, specifying among other things the minimum and maximum targets for the number of programme staff coming from each region of the world.

Of the 61 programme staff in September 1997, 9 were from Africa, 8 from Asia (including Australia and Aotearoa New Zealand), 22 from Europe, 4 from Latin America and the Caribbean, 5 from the Middle East, 12 from North America and 1 from the Pacific (the only region for which it proved impossible to meet the minimum staffing level specified). Overall, the 237 staff members in 1997 came from 52 different countries, down somewhat from the 63 countries represented among the 343 staff seven years earlier.

In terms of church traditions, the largest numbers of staff in grades 7-10 come from Reformed or Congregational churches (15), followed by Orthodox (14 – 9 Eastern Orthodox and 5 Oriental Orthodox), Lutherans (13) and Methodists (11).

Throughout this period consistent efforts have been made to improve the gender balance among WCC programme staff. In 1996, 42.4 percent of the programme staff were women, the highest percentage in the recent history of the WCC. A large number of subsequent staff departures meant that by September 1997 this has dropped to a little more than 38 percent women among programme staff.